THE WINE DIET
COOKBOOK

THE WINE DIET COOKBOOK

by Dr. Salvatore P. Lucia

Emily Chase, M.S.

Created by the Wine Advisory Board

ABELARD-SCHUMAN
An Intext Publisher
New York

Published in Association with PIPER
Blue Earth, Minnesota
San Francisco

Library of Congress Cataloging in Publication Data

Lucia, Salvatore Pablo, 1901-
   The wine diet cookbook.

   1. Wine-Therapeutic use.   2. Low-calorie diet.
I. Chase, Emily, joint author.   II. Title.
RM256.L82   641.6′2   73-18361
ISBN 0-200-04021-9

Abelard-Schuman Limited, 257 Park Avenue South, New York, N.Y. 10010, U.S.A.

Published on the same day in Canada by Longman Canada Limited.
Printed in the United States of America.

Contents

Preface

This book is dedicated to combining in a tasteful manner the glories of good food and wine with the precepts of needful restriction. We believe that those who diet have a right to enjoy all the benefits of a civilized cuisine without the penalties and burdens of unwanted girth. In presenting a daily program which is adequate both in calories and in nutritional elements essential for body growth, maintenance, and repair, the authors have sought to avoid the monotony and other punishments of the average reducing diet, and thereby preserve in a savory and entertaining fashion the unequaled pleasure of good, wholesome dining.

Salvatore P. Lucia

Introducing the Authors

Physican

Salvatore Pablo Lucia, M.D., who authored the medical sections of this book, was born in San Francisco and educated at the University of California at Berkeley. During his long and illustrious career he was a Professor (now Professor Emeritus) of Medicine and Preventive Medicine at the University of California School of Medicine, San Francisco, a lecturer on the History of Health Sciences, and currently he is practicing internal medicine.

He is the author of seven books and countless scientific articles for medical journals. Dr. Lucia, a noted enophile, has long been interested in wine as a dietary beverage and has brought California wines into medical research literature and into the modern study of the health values of wine.

Preferentially, Dr. Lucia uses the wines of California in the clinical and research aspects of his studies of the medical effects of wine on human subjects.

He is indeed superbly qualified to provide useful and basic knowledge to *The Wine Diet Cook Book.*

Home Economist

Users of this book will be pleased to know that every recipe has been tested, re-tested and tasted at meals by slimmers and non-slimmers alike. The dishes were created and cooked by Emily Chase in her own home kitchen and served to her family and friends. The tasters were always candid and sometimes critical, and dishes were carefully revised or eliminated if they did not measure up to her high standard. A frequent (and most rewarding) comment: "But it doesn't taste like a diet dish!"

Wine cookery has been Home Economist Emily Chase's specialty for over twenty years; she has two other wine cookbooks to her credit.

In this book, with Phyllis Ullman as her nutrition advisor, she has revised and in some cases entirely changed her cooking techniques to reduce the calorie content of favorite dishes, without sacrificing good eating; and the California wines she used proved an unvarying source of flavor and interest. As she said, the proof of the pudding is ahead of you, and she hopes you enjoy all the meals and achieve results on the scales.

WINE ADVISORY BOARD
San Francisco

The Role of Wine in a Reducing Diet

For untold centuries before the birth of Christ wine has been companion to food and as such, has played an important part in the function of nutrition. In ancient Greece, the frugal diet of the Spartans—those vigorous athletes and warriors —always included wine as well as barley, cheese, figs, flesh and fish. In our modern world, wine still holds its old important place in human sustenance.

However, the abundance and diversity of food available, and the elimination of much physical labor today, have led to a development historically new for great numbers of people—the frugal diet is hard to come by! If we wish to lose weight, we must limit ourselves consciously, count calories, say *no* to appetite.

To maintain good health, to say nothing of a svelte figure, almost all of us, at some time in our lives, face the necessity of imposing restrictions upon ourselves at the table. We know that wine, which is of provable benefit to the body, can be useful in a diet regimen.

If wine is introduced into the diet, very little willpower will be needed to diminish the volume of a meal. Experiments along these lines have shown that persons voluntarily and even unwittingly reduce the amount of food they eat when wine is served as part of a meal. The reduced food intake usually continues as long as wine provides its calories in substitution for other calories. In whichever manner it is employed, wine is a stimulating and a most salutary nutritional element. In order for wine to be effective, it should be included regularly in the diet, together with other healthful foods, rather than be taken sporadically and without plan, and a little wine "for thy stomach's sake" is best taken with the final meal of the day.

The nutritional value of wine can be underlined by the startling fact that wine —next to milk—is the most complex biologic fluid outside of a blood vessel. But, where milk is rather uniform in taste and in its nutritional content, wine can vary all the way from dry and tonic Champagne to deep and soothing Port. So, in addition to its diverse nutritional values, wine is blessed with a variety and complexity of flavors tailored to satisfy many varying palates.

9

How Alcohol Functions

The alcohol in wine is its main source of calculable energy. This is supplemented by sugar, which occurs in substantial amounts in some sweet wines. Contrary to requirements in other viticultural areas, any sugar in California wines must be grape sugar, as use of non-grape sugar in production of these wines is prohibited by law.

In a diet, what matters most is not that a wine, or any other food, contains one or more vital components, but rather how the body is able to make use of these components.

We Americans, being well versed in the counting of calories, are becoming aware of the different ways our bodies handle the calories from different foods. It will come as no surprise to us that alcohol is a quick-energy food, with calories that are readily burned rather than stored. Calories from carbohydrates, on the other hand, are usually stored by the body for future use. Here lies the principal value of wine as an energy food when weight loss is desired. It has been shown that alcohol may be used in place of fats or carbohydrates and that it may spare protein in the process. The metabolized alcohol in wine contributes directly not only to the maintenance of body energy but also to a general decrease in food intake accompanied by a better storage of proteins.

Table wines average about 80 calories per 100 cubic centimeters, or roughly 24 calories per ounce. Most of these calories come from their approximate 12 percent alcohol content. Dry Sherry contains about 33 calories per ounce when the label states 17% alcohol and 38 calories when the label states 20% alcohol. Dessert wines are about 41 to 45 calories when the label states 18% alcohol and 44 to 48 calories when the label states 20% alcohol.

The table on page 109 gives the general caloric value of basic wine-types. Individual wines will, of course, vary somewhat from these average figures. According to laboratory studies, 70 to 75 percent of the calories from alcohol in wine are available for work energy and body maintenance. Thus alcohol, within limits, can replace fats and carbohydrates in the diet on the basis of a one-for-one calorie trade. A reasonable amount would be 10 percent or less of the total calorie intake, with all other elements of the diet kept in normal proportion to one another.

How Sugars Function

Other sources of calories in wine are the simple sugars, principally glucose and fructose, which are usually stored by the body until their calories are needed for extra energy. Wines may contain from one fourth of one percent to as much as 10 percent of simple sugars, depending upon the type of wine.

Fructose is two and a half times sweeter than glucose. Research has shown that fructose is able to maintain and repair the liver, and that it serves as an intermediary substance in metabolism.

As for glucose, every physician recognizes that its rapid absorption and complete availability make it an immediately useful energy food. This is especially important when metabolic requirements are excessive. It is a protective agent for all body tissues, and some consider it to be the most important single nutritional factor in the prevention of fatty infiltration of the liver.

Calorie Loss in Cooking

Since wine is so often used as an ingredient in the dishes proposed for the menus offered in this book, it should be pointed out that a dry table wine will lose 85% of its original calories when subjected to sufficient heat to cause its alcohol to evaporate. All the alcohol in a cup of wine placed in a pan in a 300° oven for 10 minutes will boil off. The 15% of non-alcoholic calories remaining would include glycerin, pentose, glucose, etc.

Dessert wines with their higher count of sugar will lose all alcohol calories when heated as above, but will retain their sugar calories. However, if subjected to a high temperature for a longer period of time—a Sherry or Port baste on a ham baking in a 300° oven for one hour or more—the sugars will caramelize, thus destroying these calories too.

Wine as a Source of "Maintenance Elements"

The amounts of essential nutritional substances in wines will vary according to the conditions under which the grapes were grown, but both vitamins and minerals will be present in usable amounts in all wines.

VITAMINS: Of the several groups of vitamins, two—Vitamin P and the B-vitamin group—are present in wine in useful amounts. Vitamin P, which has only recently come to the attention of wine researchers, is known to strengthen the capillaries— those tiny blood vessels which ultimately carry nutrients to muscles and other tissues.

Of the B-vitamins, only five—thiamine, riboflavin, pyridoxine (B6), pantothenic acid, and nicotinic acid—are considered indispensable to the diet, although several others may be of some value yet to be determined. The presence of B-vitamins in wine distinguishes it from distilled liquors, and even from beer. The basic amounts vary according to the wine, and it is yeasts which add this important vitamin to the finished wines.

In a study to ascertain the Vitamin-B content of California grapes, musts, and wines, experimenters found in the finished wines 13 to 18 percent of the daily minimum requirement of riboflavin; 52 to 94 percent of the daily minimum requirement of pyridoxine; 5 to 14 percent of niacin; and 2 to 5 percent of pantothenic acid.

MINERALS: Modern wines contain in some degree all of the mineral elements necessary for the maintenance of human life, i.e., potassium, magnesium, sodium, calcium, iron, phosphorus, chlorine, sulfur, copper, manganese, zinc, iodine, and cobalt. The quantities will vary, but most wines will generally contain utilizable amounts of the more important minerals; that is to say, the first six listed.

Of these, sodium and iron merit further discussion. Sodium is important because it must be minimized in certain diets. Some sodium is always present in wine, but most wines—especially the dry table wines—have such a low content of sodium that they can safely be included in low-sodium diets. Whenever it is advisable to know the exact amount of sodium in a wine, a physician or dieter might do well to consult the producer of the wine in question.

Iron, on the other hand, can never be too plentiful. Most of the iron in wine is present in the reduced, or ferrous form, which means that it is easily absorbed from the gastrointestinal tract. Furthermore, the iron in wine has been shown to be predictably constant even in well-aged wines.

Port contains an average of 3.5 milligrams of iron per liter. Table wines are rich in iron, red wines having an average content of 6 milligrams per liter, and white wines an average of 4.7 milligrams per liter. Since the daily human requirement of elemental iron is currently set at 5.5 milligrams, wine is clearly an excellent source of this important mineral in the iron-deficient American diet.

The metabolized alcohol in wine contributes directly not only to the maintenance of body energy but also to a general decrease in food intake accompanied by a better storage of proteins.

The role of wine in a reducing diet may be summarized as follows:*
+Wine is a food; a source of energy for work and body maintenance.
+Its content of B-vitamins and minerals makes it a desirable supplementary source of these substances in the daily diet.
+Wines may be effectively incorporated into all sorts of diets, including the restrictive low-sodium diet.
+Wine can stimulate the flow of gastric juice and otherwise enhance efficient digestion.
+The tranquilizing action of wine may be strategically employed in the treatment of obesity, especially when emotional tension is a factor.

S. P. Lucia, M.D.

*For a detailed discussion of this subject see WINE AND YOUR WELL BEING by S. P. Lucia, Published in 1971 by Popular Library Inc., New York. For Dr. Lucia's discussion of wine and weight loss experiments, appetite, constituents, other use in diet, and pleasure, see page 110.

Notes on Wine Cookery Low Calorie Style

Slimming for most of us is a matter of re-educating the taste buds...of forgetting about high-calorie dishes that put on inches and getting to know their low-calorie counterparts. It means changing one's kitchen routine...forgetting the fattening things of life and learning to cook deliciously without them. It's a joy to discover that you don't need a lot of rich ingredients to make food taste good.

When one sets out on a slimming program, the broiled steak routine is fine, up to a point. Usually there comes a day when culinary boredom sets in, and this is where wine cookery, low-calorie style, enters the picture. Wine as an ingredient enhances the flavor of a dish but adds only a few calories when heat is applied and the alcohol evaporates. (See page 10.) The good-eating quality that wine contributes to "slim-cooked" dishes is invaluable in making them attractive to the palates of both dieters and non-dieters. Wine flavors low-fat meat sauces deliciously to replace rich gravies; salads sing when they're tossed with low-calorie wine dressings; simple desserts enhanced with wine are happy low-calorie meal endings.

As an accompaniment to the main course at dinner, a glass of table wine brings relaxation and satisfaction that adds greatly to the slimmer's enjoyment of the meal and lessens the feeling of gastronomic frustration that often comes with being on a diet.

In this book we have gathered recipes for all sorts of wine-cooked dishes and featured them in four weeks of luncheon and dinner menus. Most of the menus offer a choice of entrée to please individual tastes and suit the cook's convenience. In order to give a well-rounded food picture for each day, breakfast suggestions are included, too.

The Magic Number: 1200

The total daily calorie budget for these menus is approximately 1200, including a 4-ounce glass of table wine with dinner each night. We say "approximately," because many ingredients will vary in carbohydrate, protein, and fat content (the calorie-making constituents) according to season, variety, age, and size; canned, frozen, and packaged foods will also vary from brand to brand. We have consulted only the most reliable sources in arriving at our figures, and when authorities differ to any extent, we have taken an average to make our calorie counts as useful as possible.

We have selected a 1200-calorie program because at this calorie level it is possible to include the basic elements needed for good nutrition and still give the slimmer a chance to average as much as a two-pound loss per week.

In designing the menus we have tried to present three attractive, flavorful, and satisfying meals a day that will fulfill all the requirements for good nutrition as to protein, vitamins, and minerals and still stay within the framework of the 1200-calorie limit. We have attempted to hold down the intake of all fats, particularly animal (saturated) fats, which contribute to cholesterol problems. While this is not planned as a low-cholesterol book, too much blood cholesterol often goes hand in hand with overweight, so low-cholesterol features can make our menus and recipes more useful. We have restricted but not eliminated carbohydrates, because for most dieters slimming is a long-term process, and moderation, not abstinence, is the key to acceptance and success.

Rules of the Game

In planning the meals we have observed certain ground rules:

Eggs: No more than 3 whole eggs per week. Egg whites used alone are not counted, since they contain no cholesterol.

Meat: Of the 14 lunches and dinners per week, no more than 5 to feature red meat (beef or lamb, and occasionally liver or pork). Remaining 9 lunches and dinners to feature fish, poultry, or veal. The reason for restricting red meats is that they contain more animal (saturated) fat than the white meats (fish, poultry, and veal). We limit liver because although it is low in fat it is high in cholesterol, and pork because unless one uses the leanest possible cut and cooks it so that any fat has a chance to escape, a tasty pork dish is apt to be on the high-calorie side.

Fruits: At least one serving of citrus fruit, tomato, melon, or strawberries daily to take care of Vitamin C requirement.

Vegetables: Plenty of leafy, green, and yellow vegetables in the menus to take care of vitamin and mineral needs.

Cheese: Meals to include cheese (½ cup cottage cheese or 1 ounce hard cheese) 4 times per week to aid in keeping calcium balance. In addition, milk and yoghurt are used frequently in recipes.

Tailoring the Meals

Breakfast: Breakfast eaters can be divided into two groups: the conformists, who enjoy the traditional breakfast foods day after day, and the adventurers, who like something different each morning to tempt the appetite and get the day off to a good start.

If you're an adventurous breakfaster, you'll probably enjoy some of our less-usual suggestions such as *Pizza-Toast* or a frankfurter with prepared mustard. If you're a traditionalist, you can forget these in favor of one of the other menus featuring more familiar breakfast fare.

All the breakfasts are about equal, nutritionally speaking, and add up to approximately 200 calories. They include fruit, a protein dish (egg, bacon, cheese, etc.), and a breadstuff; or, fruit, cereal, and milk. Black coffee or tea complete the menu. Non-caloric sweetener can be used on the cereal or in the tea or coffee, if you wish.

The breakfast menus are interchangeable; you can enjoy any one on any day. Just remember the ground rule about eggs; no more than three per week.

Lunch: Some lunch menus feature hot entrées (stuffed zucchini, cheese tart, creamed chipped beef, etc.); others star cold dishes (jellied tuna, chicken mousse, etc.) or salads. Seafood, chicken, cheese, and, occasionally, meat furnish protein; fruit and/or vegetables are always included in one form or another; a breadstuff usually rounds out the menu. Sometimes the fruit on the menu appears as dessert; it can be enjoyed as a morning or afternoon snack, if you prefer.

The luncheon menus add up to approximately 300 calories, and are interchangeable. When you serve one of the meat entrées (featuring chipped beef, chicken livers, or ham), just remember to count it as one of the week's five meat meals.

Dinner: Most of the dinners appear as 3-course menus that start with a soup, salad, or other appetizer, but the salad can be served right along with the main course, if you wish. The entrée, featuring meat, poultry, or fish, is always accompanied by at least one vegetable; calories permitting, a serving of noodles, rice, or potato, is also included. There is always a dessert, usually fruit in one guise or another, sometimes a milk dessert (custard, cheesecake, or ice milk). Like the breakfast and lunch menus, the dinner menus are interchangeable; you can enjoy any one any day, keeping in mind the limit of five red-meat meals per week.

To repeat: Our menus have been planned and arranged within each week to conform to the ground rules given above. You can switch meals from day to day as you wish, or omit the ones that don't appeal to you, but if you menu-hop, keep the rules in mind.

Free-choice Vegetables

Remember, too, that each meal has been planned to provide foods essential to your well-being, so try not to omit anything or make too many changes. One exception: Certain low-calorie vegetables (as indicated in the menus and recipes) come under the heading of "all-you-want" vegetables, and can be substituted for each other as you wish. These include:

Bean sprouts	Parsley
Beans (green or wax)	Peppers
Cabbage	Pickles (sour or dill)
Cauliflower	Pimientos
Celery	Radishes
Cucumber	Scallions
Endive	Summer Squash (zucchini,
Escarole	pattypan, or crookneck)
Lettuce	Swiss Chard
Mushrooms	Watercress

Our daily 1200-calorie budget includes 50 calories to cover these all-you-want vegetables, including those served hot, enjoyed in salads, or used as an ingredient in our recipes. You can add an all-you-want vegetable to any of our menus without giving a thought to the calories. Raw all-you-want vegetables make an excellent free-calorie, between-meal snack.

Note to Non-Slimmers in the family: Non-slimmers will doubtless enjoy larger portions of many foods than are specified in our menus and recipes. They can also use sugar and cream with beverages, fruits, and cereals; add bread or rolls with regular margarine or butter to a menu as desired; drink milk at breakfast or lunch and have more than one glass of wine with dinner.

At the end of each day's menus, under the heading, "*Extra Foods for Non-Slimmers,*" we have also given suggestions for possible additions to the meals. We have tried to select dishes that are compatible with the dieter's menus and will not overwork the cook.

Once the slimmer has shed the desired poundage, some of these plus suggestions will also be useful in increasing the calorie budget from a reducing to a stay-as-you-weigh level.

Meet the Ingredients

A look at some of the ingredients used in developing our recipes will help you to achieve comparable results in your kitchen, both taste-wise and calorie-wise.

Wine as an ingredient is discussed on page 10. We have based our recipe-calorie figures on this material. When wine is used in a cooked dish, we count in 15% of its calories; when it is used in an uncooked dish, we include all its calories.

Diet margarine is specified in our menus and recipes, because it contains only half the calories of regular margarine (51 per tablespoon). It's easily spreadable, so as little as a half-teaspoon will give your breakfast toast a well-dressed look for only 9 calories.

Instant-blending flour, regular all-purpose flour that has been exposed to hot water or steam, is a granular flour that is used in our sauces because it blends more readily with liquid than regular flour and makes it easy to achieve a smooth sauce with little or no fat added. In our recipes we count flour at 30 calories per tablespoon.

Non-fat milk is used on cereal and as a recipe ingredient. This can be diluted evaporated skim milk, instant non-fat dry milk mixed with water, or fluid non-fat milk poured from the carton. In our recipes and menus milk (reconstituted or fluid) is calculated at 88 calories per cup. *Cultured buttermilk*, buttermilk made from pasteurized skim or part skim milk, is specified in our recipes and is counted at 100 calories per cup.

Process American or Swiss cheese is called for in a number of recipes because it melts readily and, happily for our purposes, has a slightly lower calorie count (105 calories per ounce) than natural cheese.

When you buy sliced process cheese, read the label to see whether you are getting a package of 1-ounce slices or ¾-ounce slices. They may look alike at first glance, but there's a difference of about 26 calories between each ¾-ounce slice and each 1-ounce slice. Some of our recipes call for one size, some for the other, and the calorie counts of the recipes are calculated accordingly.

We figure natural Cheddar cheese at 112 calories per ounce (approximately ¼ cup shredded cheese). Mozzarella cheese is a good calorie "bargain" at 84 calories per ounce. Grated Parmesan and Romano cheese are used frequently in our recipes and are given a calorie count of 27 per tablespoon.

Low-fat cottage cheese is specified in some of our breakfast menus and is often used at lunch. We have figured this at 200 calories per cup. Plain low-fat yoghurt, one of the key ingredients in our diet cuisine, has been counted at 120 calories per cup.

Calorie-reduced canned fruits are mentioned frequently in our menus, especially as an alternate for fresh fruit when the latter isn't in season. "Calorie-reduced" means that the fruit has been packed with a small amount of sugar, resulting in a canned product that more nearly resembles fresh fruit, calorie-wise, than fruit packed in heavy syrup. Calorie-reduced can also refer to fruit packed in water without any sugar. Calorie-reduced fruit is available under various brand names, and quite often you'll find the calorie count per half-cup serving on the label. Juice-pack canned pineapple and canned grapefruit, fruit packed in its own juice without added sugar, are favorites of ours and ideally suited to diet salads and desserts.

Some fruits, such as berries and cherries, are available frozen without sugar. Packed in plastic bags, they are good to keep on hand because you can use what you need for a meal and then return the rest to the freezer.

Vegetables are the dieter's best friend, serving as low-calorie key ingredients in many of our main dishes, as well as in salads, soups, and side dishes. Cook fresh vegetables as short a time as possible; if you've never tasted such things as zucchini, green beans, or cauliflower cooked *al dente*, give them a try and you may be in for a happy surprise. Cook frozen vegetables according to package directions, testing frequently with a fork to prevent overcooking.

When no recipe suggestion is made for a hot vegetable in a dinner menu it means the vegetable is to be served unadorned, without diet margarine or sauce. This is when spices and herbs (notably chopped parsley and chives), a few drops of lemon juice or California wine vinegar, and/or a sprinkling of *all-you-want* chopped green pepper or pimiento will add a good spark of flavor. Lemon-flavored pepper, not to mention all the various flavored salts (used in moderation), will turn a well-cooked plain vegetable into a dish to remember.

Meats should be as lean as possible. Buy the leanest you can find, trim off all possible fat before cooking, and cut off all visible fat before eating. Our recipes for simmered meats (pot roast, braised beef) call for chilling the juices after the meat is cooked so the fat will solidify and can be removed before the dish is finished.

The usual slimmer's portion of cooked beef or lamb is four ounces. You can visualize this as a piece of roast meat about the size and thickness of the palm of a woman's hand. Four ounces of a cut-up meat dish (braised beef, stew, etc.) would be about what would fit comfortably (with gravy) into a 6-ounce custard cup. If you have a small kitchen scale, you can use it until your eye gets accustomed to portion sizes. It will also be handy for weighing out hamburger patties, fish portions, etc. when you're preparing them for cooking and want to divide the meat or whatever into equal portions.

Chicken in our recipes involving a whole or quartered chicken is designated as a 2½- to 3-pound bird. Ideally for our calorie counts it would be a 2¾-pounder, but it isn't always easy to find one of that exact weight. The 2½- to 3-pound range will average out over a reasonable period of time so you won't be over- or under-caloried to any extent.

Tuna used in our recipes is diet-pack tuna, packed in water and vegetable broth without salt, or in water with salt. A 6½-ounce can is counted as 225 calories. Sizes of shellfish cans vary from brand to brand. You can buy crab in 6½-, 7½-, and 7¾-ounce cans, all holding about 1 cup. Since we can't be sure which size can you will find on your grocer's shelf, we give crabmeat in our recipes the approximate count for a 7¾-ounce can or 225 calories. Sizes of shrimp cans vary likewise; we give a 4½-ounce can (approximately 1 cup) a count of 150 calories.

Chicken stock base and beef stock base (approximately 11 calories per teaspoon) are invaluable granular seasonings for low-fat sauces. You'll find them in the spice section of your market, packed in small jars. These products serve the same purpose as bouillon cubes and are very handy seasoners. All you do is dip your measuring spoon in the jar and take out as much or as little as the recipe requires.

Bread Tray Notes

A breadstuff is included in most of our breakfast menus and frequently at lunch. Usually we suggest toast for breakfast and rye wafers, *Golden Toast Strips* (page 28), toast, or saltines for lunch. In all cases we give the calorie count for the breadstuff, including any diet margarine that accompanies it.

If you would like to vary your bread repertoire, you can use the list below and substitute one breadstuff for another. Whatever your choice, keep the total calorie count, including any diet margarine, the same as given in our menu. (Count the margarine at 17 calories per teaspoon.)

Calorie counts of bread and crackers are sometimes given on package labels for the benefit of would-be slimmers. Check labels as you market and you may find other interesting breadstuffs that are within our calorie budget and will add variety to your meals.

Breads & Crackers	Calories
Bread, commercial, sliced, 1 slice (av.)	
(white, whole wheat, rye, raisin, French)	65
Crackers	
Graham, 2½" square, 2 crackers	55
Oyster, ½ cup	60
Round, "butter" type (Ritz, Hi-Ho), 1 cracker	18
Saltine, 2" square, 4 crackers	50
Soda, 2½" square, 2 crackers	50
Wheat wafer, thin, 1 wafer	9
English muffin, ½ muffin	73
Rusk, 1 piece	50
Rye wafers, 1⅞" x 3½", 2 wafers	45
Zwieback, 1 piece	30

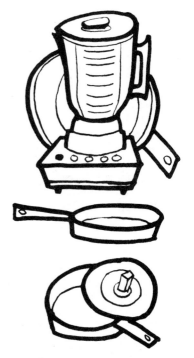

Cook's Assistants

A well-equipped kitchen is a help to any cook, and in the slimmer's kitchen there are two special musts: One or more Teflon-coated skillets and an electric blender.

We find three sizes of Teflon skillets invaluable: A small one for cooking an egg or two, a 10-inch skillet for family-sized meat, fish, and chicken dishes, and a larger one for preparing company fare for six or more. These kitchen helpers permit the browning of meat, the cooking of eggs, etc. with no or little fat. Because they are stickproof, they are a breeze to clean.

The electric blender is a wonderful help, especially in smoothing cottage cheese to sourcream consistency, whirling up salad dressing, puréeing vegetables for soups and fruits for desserts, etc. All sorts of low-calorie sleight of hand is performed swiftly and easily with the press of the blender button.

Words to Wise Slimmers

If you decide to lose weight and want to do it deliciously, let our menus and recipes show you the way. Their purpose is to help you lose pounds safely and pleasantly. When you embark on this diet, don't expect instant weight loss. Remember: Slimming takes time. Some days (or even weeks) you may not lose anything, and then be happily surprised when the scales reflect your efforts.

We believe our meals to be adequate in all food values for most people in normal health, but as is the case before starting any diet program, it's best to check with your doctor first.

We hope that you won't look on this as a diet book, but rather as a guide to enjoyable cooking and happy eating!

Emily Chase, M.S.

BIBLIOGRAPHY
(For calorie values of foods)

Bowes and Church, *Food Values of Portions Commonly Used*, eleventh edition, Philadelphia, J. B. Lippincott Company, 1970.

Kraus, Barbara, *Calories and Carbohydrates*, New York, Grosset and Dunlap, Inc., 1971.

U.S.D.A., *Nutritive Value of Foods*, Home and Garden Bulletin No. 72, revised edition, 1971.

Watt, Bernice K., Merrill, Annabel L., et. al., *Composition of Foods: Raw, Processed, Prepared*, U.S.D.A. Agriculture Handbook No. 8, revised December 1963.

28 Day's Menus with 210 Recipes for Dieters

MENU

1

(1200 calories)

BREAKFAST
(200 calories)

Half Grapefruit
(55 calories)

Canadian Bacon
*(1 ounce, 2 thin slices; pan-broil; pat with
paper towel to remove any fat / 79 calories)*

Toast
(1 slice / 65 calories)

Black Coffee or Tea

LUNCH
(300 calories)

Open-Face Salad Sandwich*
with
Seafood Dressing*

Papaya or Cantaloupe or Orange
*(½ papaya, ½ medium cantaloupe, or 1 medium
orange / 60 calories)*

Black Coffee or Tea

DINNER
(550 calories)

Relish Tray:
Radishes, Celery Hearts, Raw Cauliflowerets
*(all-you-want vegetables;
pass seasoned salt for dipping)*

Country Chicken Sauté* or Chicken-Mushroom Sauté*
or Chicken à L'Orange* or Hunter's Chicken

Carrot Purée*

Apples with Bleu Cheese Spread*

Wine Choice: CALIFORNIA ROSÉ

Extra Foods for Non-Slimmers:
(please read "Note to Non-Slimmers," page 14)

Breakfast: Slice of canned pineapple pan-broiled with
the Canadian bacon; jam or marmalade

Lunch: Potato or macaroni salad; cookies with the
fruit

Dinner: Rice with pine nuts added; another cheese or
two along with Bleu Cheese Spread, perhaps
Edam and/or Camembert

The 1200-calorie figure includes 100 calories for the 4-ounce glass of dry Table Wine and 50 calories for the *all-you-want* vegetables as listed on page 14 and used in the menus and recipes. Recipes are included for all dishes marked with an asterisk.

OPEN-FACE SALAD SANDWICH

(242 calories per serving, including dressing)

For each sandwich allow 1 slice crisp toast. Cover toast with sprigs of watercress or small, tender leaves of lettuce, or shredded lettuce *(all-you-want)*. Cover greens with thin slices of chilled, cooked zucchini or scalloped patty-pan squash *(all-you-want)*. Top squash with ½ medium tomato that has been peeled and sliced. Over the sandwich spoon ¾ cup Seafood Dressing (following). Beside sandwich on plate put a few sprigs of watercress or small lettuce leaves and 3 small or 2 large ripe olives.

All the ingredients can be prepared ahead of time, but the sandwich is best if assembled at the last minute so the toast will stay crisp.

SEAFOOD DRESSING

(192 calories per cup; 12 per tablespoon)

- 1 cup plain low-fat yoghurt
- 3 tablespoons chili sauce
- 2 tablespoons California Dry Sherry
- ½ teaspoon each: Worcestershire sauce and prepared horseradish
- 1 (7½ oz.) can (approx. 1 cup) crabmeat, 1 (6½ oz.) can diet-pack tuna, or 1½ (4½ oz.) cans (approx. 1½ cups) small shrimp
- ½ cup finely cut celery
- 1 tablespoon each: grated green pepper, chopped parsley, and chopped capers
- 1 teaspoon grated onion
  Bit of garlic, if you like
  Seasoned salt to taste

Combine yoghurt, chili sauce, Sherry, Worcestershire sauce, and horseradish in a bowl; beat with fork or small wire whisk until well blended. Add remaining ingredients; stir gently to mix.

Cover; chill an hour or more to blend flavors before serving. Makes about 2¼ cups.

COUNTRY CHICKEN SAUTÉ

(serves 4 / 388 calories per serving)

- 1 tablespoon diet margarine
- 1 (2½ to 3 lb.) frying chicken, quartered
  Sprinkling of thyme and paprika
  Salt and pepper to taste
- 4 green onions, thinly sliced (include some green tops)
  Bit of chopped or pressed garlic (optional)
- ½ cup California White Table Wine
- 1 cup drained, cooked peas
- 2 tablespoons chopped parsley

Melt margarine in large Teflon skillet. Place chicken in pan, skin side down; sauté slowly until golden brown. Turn chicken skin side up; sprinkle with thyme, paprika, salt, and pepper. Continue sautéing until chicken is brown on the underside. Add onions, garlic, and wine. Cover tightly; simmer very gently for 30 to 45 minutes, or until chicken is tender, turning pieces occasionally. Just before serving, add peas and parsley.

CHICKEN-MUSHROOM SAUTÉ

(serves 4 / 388 calories per serving)

Wipe 1 pound fresh mushrooms clean with damp sponge or cloth; remove tough portion of stems; slice mushrooms thin. Follow recipe for Country Chicken Sauté given. After chicken has simmered with the wine about 20 minutes, add mushrooms. Continue cooking until chicken is tender. No need to count extra calories, since mushrooms are an *all-you-want* vegetable.

CHICKEN À L'ORANGE

(serves 4 / 389 calories per serving)

1 tablespoon diet margarine
1 (2½ to 3 lb.) frying chicken, quartered
   Seasoned salt, pepper, and paprika
6 green onions, thinly sliced (include some
   green tops)
2 teaspoons grated orange peel
1 cup orange juice
¼ cup California Medium Sherry
2 teaspoons instant-blending flour

Melt margarine in large Teflon skillet. Place chicken in pan, skin side down; sauté slowly until golden brown. Turn chicken skin side up; sprinkle with salt, pepper, and plenty of paprika. Continue sautéing until chicken is brown on the underside. Add onions, orange peel, and orange juice. Cover tightly; simmer gently 25 minutes, turning pieces occasionally. Remove chicken from skillet. Mix Sherry and flour; add to pan juices; stir to blend sauce ingredients. Return chicken to pan; spoon sauce over. Cover; continue cooking gently 15 to 20 minutes, or until chicken is tender. Before serving, taste sauce; correct seasoning if necessary.

HUNTER'S CHICKEN

(serves 4 / 387 calories per serving)

1 tablespoon diet margarine
1 (2½ to 3 lb.) frying chicken, quartered
2 tablespoons each: chopped onion and
   green pepper
½ clove garlic, chopped or pressed
1 (8 oz.) can tomato sauce
⅓ cup California White Table Wine
   Pinch each of thyme and rosemary
   Seasoned salt and pepper to taste
1 (4 oz.) can sliced mushrooms, drained
¼ cup thinly sliced pimiento-stuffed olives
2 tablespoons chopped parsley

Melt margarine in large Teflon skillet. Place chicken in pan, skin side down; sauté slowly until golden brown. Turn chicken over; sauté until lightly browned on the underside. Add all remaining ingredients except parsley; cover; simmer gently 30 to 45 minutes, or until chicken is tender, turning and basting pieces occasionally. Before serving, taste and correct seasoning, if necessary; sprinkle with parsley.

CARROT PURÉE

(25 calories per serving)

Wash and scrape carrots. Leave whole, if small; if large, cut up. Cook in boiling salted water with 2 or 3 thin slices of onion until tender. Drain. Whirl carrots and onion in a blender, put through a ricer, or mash smooth with a potato masher. Season with salt and pepper; add a bit of chopped parsley or chives. Reheat in double boiler or over very low heat before serving. Size of portion: ½ cup.

One large carrot, cooked and mashed, will measure approximately ½ cup.

APPLES WITH BLEU CHEESE SPREAD

(131 calories per serving)

Select the best eating apples available; allow 1 apple per serving. (Or, allow ½ apple and 3 saltines per serving.) Let each person peel and slice his own apple. Pass Bleu Cheese Spread (following) for "frosting" the apple slices or crackers. Cheese Spread portion: 2 tablespoons.

BLEU CHEESE SPREAD

(28 calories per tablespoon)

4 ounces Bleu cheese (at room temperature)
1 teaspoon unflavored gelatin
½ cup skim milk
⅛ teaspoon Worcestershire sauce
   Paprika

Mash cheese thoroughly with fork. In small saucepan, mix gelatin and ¼ cup of the milk; stir over low heat 3 or 4 minutes, until gelatin is dissolved. Gradually beat gelatin mixture into cheese; beat in remaining ¼ cup milk and Worcestershire sauce. Pour into small serving bowl; chill until firm. Before serving, dust with paprika. Makes about 1 cup. This keeps very well, covered, in the refrigerator.

MENU

2

(1200 calories)

BREAKFAST
(200 calories)

Melon or Papaya
(½ small cantaloupe or papaya, or a 2-inch wedge or honeydew / 50 calories)

Deviled Egg
(shell and halve 1 hard-cooked egg; mash yolk with 1 teaspoon cottage cheese, few drops California wine vinegar, seasonings to taste; fill white halves / 84 calories)

Toast or Rye Wafers
(1 slice toast or 3 wafers / 65 calories)

Black Coffee or Tea

LUNCH
(300 calories)

Creamed Chipped Beef*
or Creamed Chipped Beef with Mushrooms*
or Chipped Beef à la King*
on Toast

Chilled Radishes and Celery Hearts
(all you want, or a hot all-you-want vegetable)

Sliced Peaches
(½ cup sliced fresh or calorie-reduced canned peaches / 33 calories)

Black Coffee or Tea

DINNER
(550 calories)

Tomato-Cucumber Salad*
with
Green Onion Dressing*

Crumb-Baked Fish Fillets*
with
Anchovy Sauce,* Caper Sauce,*
or Yoghurt Tartar Sauce*
or
Saucy Baked Fish Fillets*

Lima Beans
(½ cup cooked fresh or frozen lima beans / 99 calories)

Nectar Rosé*

Wine Choice: California Grey Riesling

Extra Foods for Non-Slimmers:

Breakfast: Slice of ham

Lunch: Marinated artichoke hearts or pickled beets on lettuce; scoop of vanilla ice milk on the peaches

Dinner: Frozen French-fried potatoes or canned shoestring potatoes with the fish; ladyfingers with dessert

The 1200-calorie figures includes 100 calories for the 4-ounce glass of dry Table Wine and 50 calories for the *all-you-want* vegetables as listed on page 14 and used in the menus and recipes. Recipes are included for all dishes marked with an asterisk.

CREAMED CHIPPED BEEF ON TOAST

(serves 2 / 266 calories per serving)

    ½ cup undiluted evaporated skim milk
    ½ cup cold water
     2 tablespoons instant-blending flour
    ½ teaspoon chicken stock base
     1 teaspoon diet margarine
     2 tablespoons shredded Cheddar cheese
     1 tablespoon California Medium Sherry
    ¼ teaspoon Worcestershire sauce
    ¼ teaspoon prepared mustard
     1 teaspoon chopped chives
     1 (3 oz.) package smoked sliced beef,
        cut up with scissors
        Seasoned salt and pepper to taste
     2 slices crisp toast

In saucepan combine evaporated milk, water, flour, and chicken stock base; stir over medium heat until mixture boils and thickens. Add margarine, cheese, Sherry, Worcestershire sauce, mustard, and chives; stir over low heat until margarine and cheese melt and blend with the sauce. Add beef to sauce; season with salt and pepper. Serve piping hot on toast. Parsley sprigs make a nice *all-you-want* garnish.

One-third cup powdered skim milk and 1 cup water can replace the evaporated milk and water here for the same calorie count.

CREAMED CHIPPED BEEF WITH MUSHROOMS

(serves 2 / 266 calories per serving)

Follow the recipe for Creamed Chipped Beef (given), but substitute liquid from 1 (4 oz.) can sliced mushrooms for part of the water. Add drained mushrooms to sauce along with chipped beef. (Or, simmer 1 heaping cup thinly sliced fresh mushrooms in ¼ cup water 5 minutes, covered; use liquid in place of part of water and add mushrooms to sauce.) Calorie count remains the same, since mushrooms are an *all-you-want* vegetable.

CHIPPED BEEF À LA KING

(serves 2 / 266 calories per serving)

Follow the recipe for Creamed Chipped Beef (given), but add 1 tablespoon each chopped green pepper and chopped pimiento to the sauce. Calorie count remains the same since pepper and pimientos are *all-you-want* vegetables. Mushrooms may also be added as in recipe above for Creamed Chipped Beef with Mushrooms.

TOMATO-CUCUMBER SALAD

(44 calories per serving, including dressing)

For each serving, line a salad plate with crisp salad greens; add thinly sliced cucumbers (any amount). Top each portion with ½ medium tomato, peeled and sliced. Just before serving, spoon 1 tablespoon Green Onion Salad Dressing (following) over all.

GREEN ONION SALAD DRESSING

(9 calories per teaspoon, 27 per tablespoon)

    ½ cup California White Table Wine
     2 tablespoons California white wine vinegar
     2 tablespoons vegetable salad oil
     1 teaspoon seasoned salt
    ½ teaspoon Worcestershire sauce
    ¼ teaspoon each: dry mustard, paprika,
        and coarse pepper
    ⅓ cup very thinly sliced green onions
        (include some green tops)

Combine all ingredients except onions in a jar or bowl; shake or beat until well blended. Add onions; mix well. Cover; chill for at least an hour to blend flavors. Shake or stir well before serving. Makes about ⅞ cup. Delightful with many mixed green and vegetable salads. Also very good with orange and grapefruit sections.

CRUMB-BAKED FISH FILLETS

(serves 3 / 262 calories per serving)

1 pound fillets of sole (thawed if frozen)
¾ cup California White Table Wine
¼ cup packaged cornflake crumbs
1½ tablespoons diet margarine, melted
  Salt, pepper, and paprika

Arrange fillets in a single layer in a baking dish; pour wine over fish; let stand 30 minutes or so. Remove fillets from wine; pat dry with paper towels. Place crumbs in a pie plate or other shallow dish. Coat fillets with crumbs, one at a time, by placing them in the dish and shaking to distribute crumbs evenly. Remove crumbed fillets to a foil-lined baking sheet. Sprinkle any remaining crumbs over fish. Drizzle melted margarine over fillets; sprinkle with salt, pepper, and paprika. Bake in 500° oven 10 to 12 minutes, or until fish flakes when tested with a fork.

Serve with one of the sauces given below, allowing 3 tablespoons sauce per portion (27 calories). Or, for the same calorie count, sprinkle with 1 tablespoon Parmesan cheese per portion instead of using sauce. Also good with lemon wedges (*all-you-want*) instead of sauce or cheese.

ANCHOVY SAUCE

(9 calories per tablespoon)

1 cup plain low-fat yoghurt
1 teaspoon anchovy paste
2 teaspoons California Dry Vermouth
1 tablespoon each: chopped chives and
  parsley

Blend yoghurt and anchovy paste; stir in remaining ingredients. Chill an hour or more to blend flavors. Makes 1 cup.

CAPER SAUCE

(9 calories per tablespoon)

Prepare Anchovy Sauce (given). Add 1 tablespoon drained capers and a sprinkling of dill weed. (Not enough added calories to count.)

YOGHURT TARTAR SAUCE

(9 calories per tablespoon)

Prepare Anchovy Sauce (given). Add 2 tablespoons finely chopped dill pickle, 1 tablespoon finely chopped capers, and 1 tablespoon finely chopped pimiento. (Not enough added calories to count.)

SAUCY BAKED FISH FILLETS

(serves 3 / 289 calories per serving)

1 pound fillets of sole (thawed if frozen)
¾ cup California White Table Wine
1 cup plain low-fat yoghurt
2 teaspoons anchovy paste
1 tablespoon chopped chives or dry
  shredded green onions
2 tablespoons packaged cornflake crumbs
  Paprika
2 tablespoons grated Parmesan cheese

Arrange fish fillets in a single layer in a shallow baking dish; pour wine over them; let stand an hour or so. Drain fillets; pat dry with paper towels; place on foil-lined baking sheet. Blend yoghurt, anchovy paste, and chives; spread mixture evenly over fillets; sprinkle with cornflake crumbs and paprika. Bake in 500° oven 10 to 12 minutes, or until fish flakes when tested with a fork. Remove from oven; sprinkle with Parmesan cheese; let stand 5 minutes or so before serving.

NECTAR ROSÉ

(serves 4 / 118 calories per serving)

½ cup California Rosé
¼ cup orange juice
1 envelope unflavored gelatin
¼ cup sugar
  Dash of salt
1 cup canned apricot nectar
1 tablespoon lemon juice

In saucepan combine wine and orange juice; sprinkle in gelatin; stir over low heat 2 to 3 minutes, until gelatin is dissolved. Stir in sugar and salt; add nectar and lemon juice. Pour into 4 dessert dishes; chill until firm. At serving time, top each portion with 1 tablespoon frozen whipped dessert topping (16 calories).

MENU
3

(1200 calories)

BREAKFAST
(200 calories)

Vegetable Juice Cocktail or Tomato Juice
(¾ cup / 35 calories)

Pizza Toast
*(spread 1 slice toast with 1 tablespoon tomato catsup;
dot with 3 cut-up anchovy fillets; sprinkle with
oregano and 2 tablespoons shredded Cheddar cheese;
bake or broil to melt cheese / 164 calories)*

Black Coffee or Tea

LUNCH
(300 calories)

Artichoke Stuffed with Shrimp*

Seafood Sauce Louise*

Golden Toast Strips*
(4 Strips / 84 calories)
or
Toast
(1 slice with 1 teaspoon diet margarine / 82 calories)

Black Coffee or Tea

DINNER
(550 calories)

Jellied Mushroom Bouillon*
Barbecued or Broiled Lamb Chops Omar*
or
Armenian Shish Kebab*

Baked or Broiled Eggplant Slices*

Baked or Broiled Tomatoes*

Rice
(½ cup cooked long-grain white rice / 91 calories)

Honeyed Pineapple*

Wine Choice: California Burgundy

Extra Foods for Non-Slimmers:

Breakfast: Crisp bacon

Lunch: Toasted English muffin; orange sherbet for
dessert

Dinner: Bread sticks with the bouillon; sliced banana
added to Honeyed Pineapple just before serving

The 1200-calorie figure includes 100 calories for the 4-ounce glass of dry Table Wine and 50 calories for the *all-you-want* vegetables as listed on page 14 and used in the menus and recipes. Recipes are included for all dishes marked with an asterisk.

ARTICHOKE STUFFED WITH SHRIMP

(215 calories per serving, including dressing)

For each serving, allow 1 large artichoke. Wash, remove outside bottom leaves, and trim off stem. Drop into plenty of boiling salted water to which you have added 1 tablespoon California wine vinegar, 1 teaspoon mixed pickling spice, and 1 clove garlic. Boil, covered, 30 to 45 minutes, or until a leaf can be pulled out easily or the bottom can be pierced easily with a fork. Turn upside down in a colander to drain and cool thoroughly. Chill covered, if time permits.

Just before serving, place artichoke on a lettuce-lined salad plate or, better still, in a shallow individual soup or cereal dish lined with lettuce. Gently spread leaves apart; pull out "cone" of smallest center leaves; remove fuzzy choke with a teaspoon. Mix ¾ cup small cooked or canned shrimp with ⅓ cup Seafood Sauce Louise (following); spoon into center of artichoke. Sprinkle with chopped parsley or paprika.

This is a finger-and-fork dish. The easiest way to eat it is to pull out a leaf with your fingers, fork a bit of salad onto the tender tip, and then enjoy it as you would any artichoke.

SEAFOOD SAUCE LOUISE
(10 calories per tablespoon, 160 per cup)

    1 cup plain low-fat yoghurt
    3 tablespoons chili sauce or catsup
    2 tablespoons California Dry Sherry
    2 tablespoons chopped parsley
    1 teaspoon grated onion
    ½ small clove garlic, chopped or pressed
    ½ teaspoon each: seasoned salt, Worcester-
       shire sauce, and prepared horseradish

Combine all ingredients in a jar or bowl: beat with a fork or small wire whisk until well blended. Cover; chill an hour or more to blend flavors. Makes 1-⅓ cups. A perfect dressing for seafood salads.

GOLDEN TOAST STRIPS

(21 calories per strip)

    2 tablespoons diet margarine
    2 tablespoons water
    ½ teaspoon chicken stock base
    ¼ teaspoon mixed Italian herbs
    6 slices white or whole wheat bread
       Paprika

In a small saucepan combine margarine, water, chicken stock base, and herbs; stir over low heat until margarine melts and chicken stock base is dissolved. With pastry brush, spread mixture over bread slices. Cut each slice in 4 strips; place on baking sheet. Bake in 250° to 275° oven 1 to 1½ hours, or until crisp and pale golden color. Remove from oven; sprinkle with paprika. When cool, store in tightly covered tin. Makes 24 strips.

JELLIED MUSHROOM BOUILLON
(serves 4 / 36 calories per serving)

    1 (4 oz.) can mushroom stems and pieces
    1 envelope unflavored gelatin
    1 (10½ oz.) can condensed chicken broth
    ½ cup water
    2 tablespoons chopped onion
    ¼ cup California Dry Sherry
    ¼ teaspoon Worcestershire sauce
       Dash of Tabasco sauce
       Salt and pepper to taste
    1 tablespoon chopped parsley
    4 lemon wedges

Drain mushrooms, reserving liquid; chop mushrooms fine. Soften gelatin in the mushroom liquid. Combine chicken broth, water, and onion in a saucepan; bring to a boil; simmer, covered, 5 minutes; strain. Add softened gelatin and Sherry to the hot broth; stir until gelatin is dissolved; add seasonings. Cool, then chill. When mixture begins to thicken, stir in mushrooms; chill until firm. At serving time, break up mixture with a fork; spoon into bouillon cups or sauce dishes; sprinkle each serving with some of the parsley and accompany with a lemon wedge.

BARBECUED OR BROILED LAMB CHOPS OMAR

(serves 4 / 244 calories per serving)

8 small loin lamb chops, cut 1 inch thick
 and trimmed of as much fat as possible
 (approx. 5 ounces each before trimming)
1 medium-sized onion, thinly sliced
1 green pepper, cut in thin strips
1 cup California White Table Wine
1 clove garlic, chopped or pressed
1 teaspoon oregano
1 teaspoon salt
½ teaspoon coarse black pepper

Arrange chops in a shallow baking dish; cover with onion slices and green pepper strips. Mix remaining ingredients; pour over chops. Let stand in the refrigerator at least 5 hours, preferably overnight, turning chops occasionally. Remove chops from marinade. Barbecue to the desired degree of doneness (or place on rack and broil in oven). Enjoy the lean portion only for this calorie count.

ARMENIAN SHISH KEBAB

(serves 4 / 240 calories per serving)

1½ pounds boned leg of lamb (as lean as
 possible), cut in 1½-inch cubes*
1 large onion, thinly sliced
2 green peppers, cut in 1-inch squares
¾ cup California Dry Vermouth
1 clove garlic, chopped or pressed
1 teaspoon salt
½ teaspoon coarse black pepper
¾ teaspoon oregano

Put meat in a bowl; add onion and green peppers. Mix remaining ingredients; pour over meat; stir well. Let stand in refrigerator several hours or overnight, stirring occasionally. An hour or so before serving time, remove from refrigerator; string meat cubes on metal skewers alternately with pieces of green pepper. Barbeque until done as you like your lamb, or broil in the oven. Serve on the skewers.

Most markets sell only a whole leg of lamb, boned, so you will probably have to buy 3½ pounds or more of boned meat. Weigh out what you need for this recipe and freeze the remainder for another time. Of course, if you are having a group for dinner, you can use all the meat and increase the other ingredients accordingly.

BAKED OR BROILED EGGPLANT SLICES

(serves 4 / 55 calories per serving)

Wash a medium-sized eggplant (about 1¼ pounds) but do not peel it; cut crosswise in ½-inch slices. Brush slices on both sides with a mixture of 2 tablespoons melted diet margarine and 2 tablespoons California Dry Vermouth; sprinkle with seasoned salt and pepper. Place on Teflon baking sheet. Bake in 400° oven 15 to 20 minutes, turning once. Or, broil until nicely browned on one side, then turn and brown on the other side. Before serving, sprinkle with paprika.

BAKED OR BROILED TOMATOES

(25 calories per serving)

For each serving, allow ½ medium-sized tomato. Cut tomatoes crosswise in halves; sprinkle cut surfaces with onion salt, pepper, and a bit of oregano, if you like. Dot each half with ½ teaspoon diet margarine. Bake in 400° oven 15 to 20 minutes, until thoroughly heated. Or, broil, cut side up, for 6 to 8 minutes.

HONEYED PINEAPPLE

(100 calories per serving)

For each serving, allow ¾ cup diced fresh pineapple (or ½ cup drained juice-pack canned pineapple chunks), 1 teaspoon each honey and lime juice, and 2 teaspoons Muscatel or Sweet Sherry. Mix lightly; cover and chill thoroughly. Serve in sherbet glasses or dessert dishes. Garnish each serving with a sprig of mint.

MENU
4
(1200 calories)

BREAKFAST
(200 calories)

Sliced Orange
(1 medium orange / 60 calories)

Shrimp on Toast
*(1/3 cup small cooked or canned shrimp mixed with
2 tablespoons plain low-fat yoghurt, a sprinkling
of chives, lemon pepper, and other seasonings to taste;
serve on 1 slice toast spread with ½ teaspoon
diet margarine / 139 calories)*

Black Coffee of Tea

LUNCH
(300 calories)

Curried Chicken Mousse*
with
Fruit Salad and Amber Dressing
or
Vegetable Salad and Tangy Dressing

Rye Wafers or Golden Toast Strips
(3 wafers or 3 Strips, page 28 / 63 calories)

Black Coffee or Tea

DINNER
(550 calories)

Tomato and Green Bean Salad*
with Bleu Cheese Dressing*
Zucchini-Beef Casserole Italienne*
or
Beef and Spinach Casserole Trieste*

Polenta
*(2/3 cup cooked cornmeal mixed with 2 teaspoons
grated Parmesan cheese / 98 calories)*

Baked Applesauce Crisp*

Wine Choice: California Barbera

Extra Foods for Non-Slimmers:

Breakfast: Apricot nectar as a sauce over the orange

**Lunch: Celery stuffed with a blend of Neufchatel
cheese, chopped chutney, and milk or cream
to make a spreadable mixture; brownies for
dessert**

**Dinner: French bread; scoop of vanilla ice milk on
Baked Applesauce Crisp**

The 1200-calorie figure includes 100 calories for the 4-ounce glass of dry Table Wine and 50 calories for the *all-you-want* vegetables as listed on page 14 and used in the menus and recipes. Recipes are included for all dishes marked with an asterisk.

CURRIED CHICKEN MOUSSE

(serves 4 / 149 calories per serving)

1   envelope unflavored gelatin
¼   cup California White Table Wine
2   chicken bouillon cubes
1   cup boiling water
1   tablespoon lemon juice
1   teaspoon grated onion
½   teaspoon each: dry mustard and curry powder
½   teaspoon Worcestershire sauce
1   cup plain low-fat yoghurt
    Salt and/or garlic salt to taste
1½ cups finely diced, cooked chicken
½   cup finely diced celery
1   tablespoon each: chopped green pepper, pimiento, and parsley

In mixing bowl, soften gelatin in wine 5 minutes. Dissolve bouillon cubes in boiling water; add to gelatin, stirring until dissolved. Add lemon juice, onion, mustard, curry powder, and Worcestershire sauce; stir well. Cool 5 minutes. Add yoghurt; beat with rotary beater or wire whisk until ingredients are smoothly blended. Season with salt and/or garlic salt to taste. Chill until mixture is consistency of unbeaten egg white; fold in remaining ingredients. Spoon into 4 individual molds or custard cups that have been rinsed with cold water; chill until firm.

At serving time, line a luncheon plate with crisp salad greens *(all-you-want)*; unmold Curried Chicken Mousse on greens alongside a serving of Fruit Salad (following); spoon Amber Fruit Salad Dressing (page 70) over fruit. Or, accompany the Mousse with a serving of Vegetable Salad (following) and spoon Tangy Dressing (page 43) over vegetables.

Fruit Salad: (89 calories per serving, including dressing) For each serving, allow 1 slice juice-pack canned pineapple and ½ cup drained water-pack canned mandarin oranges. Place pineapple on greens; top with orange segments; spoon 1 tablespoon Amber Dressing over fruit. Sprinkle a little finely chopped green pepper over fruit for extra color and flavor. Makes 1 pint.

Vegetable Salad: (89 calories per serving, including dressing. For each serving, allow ½ medium tomato, 2 medium spears cooked broccoli, and 2 canned (not marinated) or cooked frozen artichoke hearts. Place tomato on greens; top with broccoli spears; add artichoke hearts, cut in halves or thirds if whole. Spoon 4 teaspoons Tangy Dressing (page 43) over vegetables. Garnish with a strip or two of pimiento.

TOMATO AND GREEN BEAN SALAD, BLEU CHEESE DRESSING

(58 calories per serving, including dressing)

For each serving, allow ½ medium tomato, all the chilled cooked or canned green beans and salad greens you wish, and 2 tablespoons Bleu Cheese Dressing (following). Line a salad plate with crisp greens; top with peeled tomato half; top tomato with green beans. Spoon Bleu Cheese Dressing over salad; garnish with 1 rolled anchovy fillet.

BLEU CHEESE DRESSING

(17 calories per tablespoon)

¼   cup cold water
⅓   cup powdered non-fat milk
1½ cups low-fat cottage cheese
3   tablespoons (1½ oz.) crumbled Bleu cheese
1   clove garlic
2   tablespoons lemon juice
1   tablespoon California white wine vinegar
¼   teaspoon Worcestershire sauce
1   teaspoon seasoned salt
½   teaspoon lemon pepper
1   tablespoon chopped chives

Combine all ingredients except chives in blender; whirl until smooth. Turn into jar or bowl; stir in chives; cover and chill at least 1 hour before using. A delicious dressing that keeps very well. Makes 1 pint.

ZUCCHINI-BEEF CASSEROLE ITALIENNE

(serves 6 / 253 calories per serving)

1 pound ground beef (as lean as possible)
½ cup chopped onion
1 clove garlic, chopped or pressed
3 (8 oz.) cans tomato sauce
1 cup California Red Table Wine
1 teaspoon mixed Italian seasoning
¼ teaspoon allspice
1 bay leaf, crumbled
  Seasoned salt and pepper to taste
1 (4 oz.) can sliced mushrooms, drained,
  or 1 heaping cup sliced fresh mushrooms,
  simmered, covered, in ¼ cup water 5
  minutes and drained
2 pounds small zucchini (10 to 12 squash)
¼ pound (4 oz.) shredded Mozzarella
  cheese
2 tablespoons grated Parmesan cheese

In Teflon skillet, sauté beef, onion, and garlic together until meat is nicely browned, stirring with fork to separate it into bits. Drain off all fat from skillet. To meat mixture add tomato sauce, wine, and seasonings; mix well. Cover; simmer gently 1 hour, stirring frequently. Add mushrooms. While meat sauce is cooking, wash zucchini and trim off ends; do not peel. Cook, whole, in boiling salted water about 10 minutes, or just until barely tender; drain. When cool enough to handle, cut lengthwise in halves; arrange, cut side up, in single layer in shallow baking dish. Sprinkle zucchini with Mozzarella cheese; pour meat sauce over it; sprinkle with Parmesan cheese. Bake in 350° oven 45 minutes.

BEEF AND SPINACH CASSEROLE TRIESTE

(serves 6 / 254 calories per serving)

1 pound ground beef (as lean as possible)
½ cup chopped onion
1 clove garlic, chopped or pressed
1 (8 oz.) can tomato sauce
⅓ cup California Red Table Wine
1 (4 oz.) can sliced mushrooms, drained,
  or 1 heaping cup sliced fresh mushrooms, simmered, covered in ¼ cup
  water 5 minutes and drained
1 teaspoon dried basil
  Pinch of oregano
  Salt and pepper to taste
1 (10 oz.) package frozen chopped
  spinach
¾ cup low-fat cottage cheese
1 tablespoon grated Parmesan cheese
¼ pound (4 oz. shredded Mozzarella
  cheese
  Paprika

In Teflon skillet, sauté beef, onion, and garlic together until meat is nicely browned, stirring with fork to separate it into bits. Drain off all fat from skillet. To meat mixture add tomato sauce, wine, mushrooms, and seasonings; mix well. Cover; simmer 10 minutes, stirring several times. Uncover; simmer a few minutes longer, until mixture is quite thick and no longer "saucy."

Cook spinach according to package directions; turn spinach into strainer and press with rubber spatula or back of spoon to drain thoroughly. Mix spinach, cottage cheese, and Parmesan cheese; season with salt and pepper; spread in baking dish (8 by 8 by 2 inches) greased with ⅛ teaspoon diet margarine. Spoon meat sauce over spinach mixture; sprinkle with Mozzarella cheese; dust with paprika. Bake in 375° oven 20 minutes, or until bubbly. Remove from oven; let settle a few minutes before serving.

BAKED APPLESAUCE CRISP

(serves 6 / 126 calories per serving)

3 cups unsweetened applesauce (a 1-lb. can
  plus an 8-oz. can)
1 teaspoon cinnamon
½ teaspoon each: orange peel
  and lemon peel
½ cup cornflake crumbs
¼ cup brown sugar
2 tablespoons diet margarine, melted

Mix applesauce, cinnamon, orange peel, and lemon peel; spread in 9-inch pie plate. Mix cornflake crumbs, brown sugar, and margarine; sprinkle evenly over applesauce; pat down gently but firmly. Bake in 375° oven 30 minutes. Serve warm or chilled. Top each portion with 1 tablespoon frozen whipped dessert topping (16 calories).

MENU
5
(1200 calories)

BREAKFAST
(200 calories)

Tomato Yoghurt Shake
*(in pint jar shake together 1 cup chilled tomato juice
or vegetable juice cocktail, ½ cup plain low-fat
yoghurt, 2 teaspoons lemon juice,
¼ teaspoon Worcestershire sauce, and salt to
taste / 106 calories)*

Toast with Deviled Ham
(2 teaspoons deviled ham on 1 slice toast / 95 calories)

Black Coffee or Tea

LUNCH
(300 calories)

Italian Country Soup* or Curried Zucchini Soup*
and
Parmesan Toast*
or
Casserole Onion Soup
with Toast and Cheese Topping*

Crisp Radishes and Celery Hearts
(all-you-want)

Cantaloupe or Pear
*(½ small cantaloupe or ½ cup fresh or calorie-reduced
canned pear slices / 50 calories)*

Black Coffee or Tea

DINNER
(550 calories)

Venetian Spinach Salad*
Veal Sauté with Mushrooms*

Artichoke Hearts
*(½ cup cooked frozen hearts, ⅓ of a 9-oz. package)
seasoned with garlic salt and a sprinkling of
lemon juice / 22 calories)*

Noodles
*(½ cup cooked wide noodles, mixed with ½ teaspoon
diet margarine / 109 calories)*

Jellied Vin Café*

Wine Choice: California Dry Sauterne

Extra Foods for Non-Slimmers:

Breakfast: Poached or fried egg on top of Deviled Ham
Toast, or top toast with shredded Cheddar
cheese and broil briefly

Lunch: Cherry tomatoes and olives on the relish tray;
gingersnaps with the fruit

Dinner: Crumbled crisp bacon or bacon-flavored bits
on the salad; rice or noodles with the veal;
trickle of California Vin Café over the dessert
topping

The 1200-calorie figure includes 100 calories for the 4-ounce glass of dry Table Wine and 50 calories for the *all-you-want* vegetables as listed
on page 14 and used in the menus and recipes. Recipes are included for all dishes marked with an asterisk.

CURRIED ZUCCHINI SOUP

(serves 3 / 117 calories per serving)

1 pound zucchini
2 tablespoons diet margarine
2 tablespoons sliced green onions
1 clove garlic, sliced
¼ cup California Dry Vermouth
½ teaspoon curry powder
½ teaspoon salt
1¾ cups canned condensed chicken broth
⅓ cup powdered non-fat milk
Chopped parsley or chives

Scrub zucchini; trim off ends but do not peel; slice thin. Melt margarine in skillet; add zucchini, onions, garlic, and Vermouth. Stir over medium-high heat until mixture becomes steamy; cover, turn heat low, and simmer 10 minutes. Shake pan occasionally; do not let vegetables brown. Spoon mixture (including any liquid) into blender; add seasonings and chicken broth; whirl 30 seconds. Pour mixture into saucepan; blend in powdered milk; heat thoroughly but do not allow to boil. Before serving, taste and check seasoning. Pour into heated soup bowls; sprinkle with a little parsley or chives. Makes about 4 cups. This soup is also delicious served chilled.

PARMESAN TOAST

(serves 3 /136 calories per serving)

Mix ½ cup plain low-fat yoghurt, 6 tablespoons grated Parmesan cheese, 1 tablespoon finely chopped green onion, ½ teaspoon Worcestershire sauce, ¼ teaspoon prepared mustard, and salt to taste. Toast 3 slices bread on one side; spread cheese mixture on untoasted side. Bake in 450° oven about 10 minutes, or until bubbly and browned. Or, broil 4 to 6 minutes, watching carefully! Let cool a minute before serving.

ITALIAN COUNTRY SOUP

(serves 6 / 119 calories per serving)

2 tablespoons diet margarine
1 cup each: diced raw carrot, zucchini, celery, and onion
1 cup shredded cabbage
1 cup cut green beans
½ green pepper, diced
¼ cup snipped parsley sprigs
1 clove garlic, chopped or pressed
¼ cup California Dry Vermouth
1 (1 lb.) can stewed tomatoes
2 (10½ oz.) cans condensed bouillon (beef broth)
2½ cups water
1 cup California Red Table Wine
3 teaspoons (1 tablespoon) beef stock base
½ teaspoon mixed Italian seasoning
2 teaspoons Worcestershire sauce
1 bay leaf (whole)
Salt and pepper to taste
6 tablespoons grated Parmesan cheese

Melt margarine in Dutch oven or other heavy kettle; add carrot, zucchini, celery, onion, cabbage, beans, green pepper, parsley, garlic, and Vermouth. Stir over medium-high heat until mixture is steamy; cover, turn heat low, and simmer 10 minutes, stirring frequently. Do not let vegetables brown. Add remaining ingredients except cheese; cover; simmer gently 1½ hours, stirring occasionally. Before serving, remove bay leaf; taste and adjust seasoning, if necessary. Pour into heated soup bowls; sprinkle 1 tablespoon Parmesan cheese over each serving. Makes about 9 cups.

CASSEROLE ONION SOUP

(serves 4 / 252 calories per serving, including toast and cheese)

      1 tablespoon diet margarine
      3 cups thinly sliced yellow onions
    ½ cup California Dry Vermouth
      2 (10½ oz.) cans condensed consommé
    2½ cups water
    ½ cup California White Table Wine
         Salt to taste
      4 slices dry toasted French bread
      1 cup grated Parmesan cheese

Melt margarine in saucepan; add onion and Vermouth. Stir over medium-high heat until mixture is steamy; cover, turn heat low, and cook 5 minutes, stirring several times. Add consommé, water, white wine, and salt; bring to boil; turn heat very low and cook, uncovered, for 3 hours, stirring occasionally. Heat should be kept low enough so that liquid is barely bubbling. Pour soup into 4 individual casseroles (2-cup capacity); float slices of toast on top; sprinkle each slice with ¼ cup cheese. Bake in 350° oven 30 minutes. Remove from oven; let stand a few minutes before serving because soup will be very, very hot. Makes about 5½ cups.

VENETIAN SPINACH SALAD

(serves 4 / 50 calories per serving)

To serve 4, allow 3 cups chilled bite-size pieces of crisp, tender spinach, 3 snipped anchovy fillets, 2 thinly sliced green onions, and 4 tablespoons (¼ cup) Venetian Salad Dressing (following). Toss together just before serving.

VENETIAN SALAD DRESSING

(11 calories per teaspoon, 33 per tablespoon)

    ½ cup California White Table Wine
      2 tablespoons vegetable salad oil
      2 tablespoons lemon juice
      2 tablespoons grated Parmesan cheese
      2 tablespoons chopped parsley
    ½ clove garlic, chopped or pressed
    ½ teaspoon salt
    ¼ teaspoon Worcestershire sauce
    ¼ teaspoon each: sugar, paprika, and
         coarse pepper

Combine all ingredients in jar or bowl; shake or beat to mix well. Chill, covered, for at least an hour to blend flavors. Always shake or beat well before serving. Makes ¾ cup. Good with any mixed green salad, but especially fine with those that include spinach.

VEAL SAUTÉ WITH MUSHROOMS

(serves 3 / 281 calories per serving)

    ½ pound fresh mushrooms
      1 pound veal round steak, cut ½ inch thick
      1 tablespoon flour
      1 tablespoon diet margarine
      1 clove garlic, chopped or pressed
         Salt, pepper, and paprika to taste
         Dash each of thyme and marjoram
    ½ teaspoon chicken stock base
    ½ teaspoon grated lemon peel
    ½ teaspoon Worcestershire sauce
      2 tablespoons chopped parsley
    ½ cup California White Table Wine
    ½ cup water
      2 tablespoons California Dry Sherry

Wipe mushrooms with damp sponge or cloth; remove tough portion of stems; slice mushrooms thin; set aside. Remove skin and bone from veal; with meat tenderizer, mallet, or edge of heavy plate, pound veal until ¼ inch thick; cut in manageable pieces. Sprinkle flour on sheet of waxed paper; dip veal in flour, turning to coat both sides.

Melt margarine in 10-inch Teflon skillet; add garlic; cook a minute or two. Arrange veal in skillet in single layer; sauté over medium heat until browned on one side, then turn and brown on the other side. Sprinkle with salt, pepper, paprika, thyme, marjoram, and chicken stock base. Add lemon peel and Worcestershire sauce. Scatter mushrooms and parsley over veal; add white wine and water. Cover; simmer gently about 45 minutes, or until veal is fork-tender, turning pieces frequently and adding a little water if needed to keep gravy a nice consistency. Before serving, add Sherry; taste and correct seasoning if necessary.

JELLIED VIN CAFÉ

(serves 4 / 69 calories per serving)

Soften 1 envelope unflavored gelatin in ½ cup cold water. In saucepan combine 1 cup water, 3 tablespoons sugar, dash of salt, 1 (3-inch) stick cinnamon, and 3 whole cloves. Bring to boil; simmer 5 minutes. Remove cinnamon and cloves. To hot liquid add softened gelatin, 2 tablespoons instant coffee powder, and ¼ cup California Vin Café; stir until coffee and gelatin are dissolved. Pour into 4 dessert dishes; chill until firm. At serving time, top each portion with 1 tablespoon frozen whipped dessert topping (16 calories). A dusting of cinnamon can go over the topping without extra calories.

MENU
6
(1200 calories)

BREAKFAST
(200 calories)

Half Grapefruit
(55 calories)

Melted Cheese on Toast
(1 slice toast and a ¾ oz. slice process American cheese; spread toast with prepared mustard; top with cheese; bake or broil to melt cheese / 145 calories)

Black Coffee or Tea

LUNCH
(300 calories)

Salad Plate:

Stuffed Tomato with Shrimp or Crabmeat*

Yoghurt Dressing I* or II*

Dill Bean and Mushroom Relish*

Golden Toast Strips or Rye Wafers
(3 Strips, page 28, or 3 wafers / 63 calories)

Raw Apple or Applesauce
(1 medium apple; or ½ cup canned unsweetened applesauce plus 1½ teaspoons sugar and cinnamon to taste / 75 calories)

Black Coffee or Tea

DINNER
(550 calories)

Celery Bouillon*

Liver Sauté with Smothered Onions*

—or—

Liver and Mushrooms Sauté*

Broccoli
(2 medium spears or ⅔ cup chopped, seasoned with lemon juice / 30 calories)

Baked Potato
(1 medium, 3-to-a-lb.; fluff with 2 tablespoons skim milk; omit skin / 103 calories)

**Melon or Apricot Cup with
Orange-Port Sauce***

Wine Choice: California Burgundy

Extra Foods for Non-Slimmers:

Breakfast: Vienna sausages or crisp bacon

Lunch: Bleu or Cheddar cheese with the apple or a dollop of frozen whipped dessert topping on the applesauce

Dinner: Crackers with the bouillon; sour half and half on the baked potato; cup cake with the fruit

The 1200-calorie figure includes 100 calories for the 4-ounce glass of dry Table Wine and 50 calories for the *all-you-want* vegetables as listed on page 14 and used in the menus and recipes. Recipes are included for all dishes marked with an asterisk.

STUFFED TOMATO WITH SHRIMP OR CRABMEAT

(158 calories per serving, including dressing)

For each serving, allow 1 medium-sized tomato, ½ (4½ oz.) can small shrimp (approximately ½ cup) or ⅓ (7½ oz.) can crabmeat (approximately ⅓ cup). Peel tomato and cut almost through in 6 or 8 sections; place on a lettuce-lined plate and gently spread sections apart. Mix shrimp or crabmeat with finely cut raw or briefly-cooked celery to taste; add Yoghurt Dressing I or II (following) to bind the mixture; heap in tomatoes. Sprinkle with paprika or chopped parsley. Pass additional Yoghurt Dressing with the salad. Dressing portion for this dish is 5 tablespoons, including what's mixed in and spooned over it. The lettuce and celery are *all-you-want* ingredients.

YOGHURT DRESSING I

(10 calories per tablespoon)

  4 teaspoons chicken stock base
  2 tablespoons California Dry Vermouth
  1 pint (2 cups) plain low-fat yoghurt
  1 teaspoon lemon juice
  1 teaspoon Worcestershire sauce
  ¼ teaspoon dry mustard
  2 teaspoons chopped chives or dry
    shredded green onions
    Pinch of dill weed
    Chopped or pressed garlic to taste
    Seasoned salt to taste

Dissolve chicken stock base in wine; add to yoghurt; blend well with a fork or wire whisk. Stir in remaining ingredients. Turn into a pint jar; cover and chill at least an hour so flavors can mingle before serving. Makes 2 cups. A creamy, flavorful dressing that keeps well. Excellent with vegetable, seafood, and chicken salads.

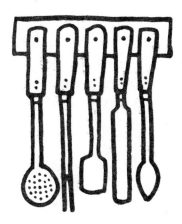

YOGHURT DRESSING II

(9 calories per tablespoon)

  1 pint (2 cups) plain low-fat yoghurt
  2 tablespoons California Dry Vermouth
  1 teaspoon Dijon prepared mustard
  2 teaspoons chopped chives or dry
    shredded green onion
1½ teaspoons seasoned salt (or to taste)
  1 teaspoon Worcestershire sauce
  1 teaspoon lemon juice
  1 teaspoon grated onion
  1 small clove garlic, chopped or pressed

Combine all ingredients in a jar or bowl; beat with fork or small wire whisk until well blended. Cover; chill at least an hour to blend flavors. (Overnight chilling is even better.) Makes 2 cups. Delicious wherever a creamy dressing would be used. This keeps very well in the refrigerator.

CELERY BOUILLON

(serves 3 / 26 calories per serving)

Combine in a saucepan 1 (10½ oz.) can bouillon (beef broth), ¾ cup water, ½ cup finely cut heart of celery, and 4 whole cloves. Cover; simmer gently 5 minutes. Remove cloves. Stir in 3 tablespoons California Dry Sherry; heat another minute or so. Add salt and / or onion salt to taste. Pour piping hot into heated soup cups; add a thin slice of lemon and 1 teaspoon chopped parsley to each cup.

DILL BEAN AND MUSHROOM RELISH

(Serves 4 or more / too few calories to count, since these are all-you-want vegetables)

- ¼ **pound fresh mushrooms**
- 1 **(1 lb.) can vertical-pack whole green beans**
- 1 **teaspoon dill seed**
- 5 **whole peppercorns**
- 1 **bay leaf**
- ⅔ **cup California white wine tarragon vinegar**
- ⅓ **cup California Dry Vermouth**
- 1 **clove garlic, chopped or pressed**
- 2 **teaspoons seasoned salt**
- 1 **cup cold water**

Wipe mushrooms with damp sponge or cloth; cut off tough portion of stems; slice mushrooms thin; set aside. Drain beans; rinse with cold water; drain again. Pack beans carefully into a 1-quart jar, keeping them as upright as possible. Drop in mushrooms; add dill seed, peppercorns, and bay leaf. In saucepan combine vinegar, wine, garlic, and salt; heat to simmering. Remove from heat; add cold water; pour over beans and mushrooms. Put lid on jar; refrigerate at least 24 hours, gently turning jar occasionally to distribute seasonings. To serve, drain vegetables; place on lettuce-lined plate or in shallow bowl. Chopped parsley or a strip or two of pimiento makes a good no-calorie-to-count garnish. This relish is an excellent keeper.

LIVER SAUTÉ WITH SMOTHERED ONIONS

(serves 3 / 289 calories per serving)

- ¾ **pound (12 oz.) beef or calf liver, sliced about ¼" thick**
- 2 **cups thinly sliced onions, separated into rings**
- ½ **cup California Red Table Wine**
- ¼ **cup water**
- 1 **teaspoon beef stock base**
- ½ **teaspoon Worcestershire sauce**
  Seasoned salt, pepper, and paprika to taste

Remove thin outside skin from liver slices. Combine onions, ¼ cup wine, and water in a large Teflon skillet; sprinkle with beef stock base and Worcestershire sauce; stir well. Cook, stirring, over medium heat until mixture becomes steamy; cover pan and simmer gently for 10 to 15 minutes, or until onions are tender. Stir several times and add a little more water if needed to keep pan from becoming dry. (Not too much water, because when onions are tender, liquid should have evaporated.) Remove cooked onions from pan and set aside. Place liver

in the warm pan; sprinkle with salt, pepper, and paprika. Cook over medium-high heat just until lightly browned on the underside, then turn, season, and brown the other side. Don't overcook or the liver will lose its juicy tenderness. About a minute on each side should do the trick. Remove liver to heated dinner plates. Return onions to pan; add remaining ¼ cup wine; quickly swish onions around in the pan to reheat them, then spoon over liver.

LIVER AND MUSHROOMS SAUTÉ

(serves 3 / 290 calories per serving)

- ½ **pound fresh mushrooms**
- ¾ **pound beef or calf liver, sliced about ¼ inch thick**
- 1 **tablespoon flour**
- 1½ **tablespoons diet margarine**
- ¼ **cup finely chopped onion**
- 1 **teaspoon beef stock base**
- ¼ **cup water**
- ¼ **cup California Dry Sherry**
- 1 **teaspoon Worcestershire sauce**
  Dash of thyme
  Seasoned salt and pepper to taste
- 2 **tablespoons chopped parsley**

Wipe mushrooms with damp cloth or sponge; remove tough portion of stems; slice mushrooms thin. Set mushrooms aside. Remove thin outside skin from liver slices. Spread flour in a pie plate or other shallow dish; dip liver slices in flour, coating both sides. Cut slices in halves or thirds. Melt margarine in a 10-inch Teflon skillet; add liver in a single layer; sauté over medium-high heat just until lightly browned on the underside, then turn and brown the other side. Don't overcook! Remove liver from skillet. Combine mushrooms and onion in the skillet; sprinkle with beef stock base; add water. Stir over medium-high heat until mixture becomes steamy, then cover, turn heat low, and cook 5 minutes, shaking pan frequently. Add Sherry; season with Worcestershire sauce, thyme, salt, and pepper. Just before serving, add liver to skillet; heat until mixture is piping hot, no longer. Serve at once, sprinkled with chopped parsley.

MELON OR APRICOT CUP WITH ORANGE-PORT SAUCE

(101 calories per serving)

For each serving, allow ¾ cup diced cantaloupe, casaba, or honeydew melon, or ½ cup fresh or calorie-reduced canned apricot halves; 2 tablespoons orange juice; and 2 tablespoons California Red or White Port. Combine ingredients in bowl; add a few gratings of fresh orange peel. Mix lightly; chill thoroughly before serving.

BREAKFAST
(200 calories)

Tomato Juice
(¾ cup / 35 calories)

Crisp Bacon
(2 medium slices, baked on rack in shallow pan, 400° oven, 15 to 20 minutes / 92 calories)

Toast
(1 piece with ½ teaspoon diet margarine / 74 calories)

Black Coffee or Tea

LUNCH
(300 calories)

Vineyard Cheese Tart* or Chili-Cheese Tart*

Pineapple Cocktail Salad*

Black Coffee or Tea

DINNER
(550 calories)

Jellied Chicken Loaf* with Egg Dressing*
or
Buffet Halibut Loaf* with Cucumber Dressing*

Chilled Vegetable Platter Salad
(center lettuce-lined platter with whole, cooked cauliflower; surround with cooked green beans and / or zucchini strips; add pimiento strips for color / an all-you-want salad)
with White Wine Dressing
(page 79; 2 tablespoons per portion / 60 calories)

Sliced Tomatoes with Herbs*

Golden Toast Strips
(page 28; 3 Strips / 63 calories)

Vanilla Ice Milk with Crushed Strawberries
(½ cup ice milk and ⅓ cup capped fresh or unsweetened frozen berries / 160 calories)

Wine Choice: California Chablis

Extra Foods for Non-Slimmers:

Breakfast: Peanut butter to spread on the toast; jam or jelly

Lunch: Frozen or instant chocolate pudding with frozen whipped dessert topping

Dinner: Marinated artichoke hearts and ripe olives; heated French rolls; individual meringue or sponge-cake cup under the dessert

The 1200-calorie figure includes 100 calories for the 4-ounce glass of dry Table Wine and 50 calories for the *all-you-want* vegetables as listed on page 14 and used in the menus and recipes. Recipes are included for all dishes marked with an asterisk.

VINEYARD CHEESE TART

(serves 6 / 220 calories per serving)

- 3 eggs
- 1 cup California White Table Wine
- 1 cup water
- 2 teaspoons chicken stock base
- 1 teaspoon Worcestershire sauce
- ½ teaspoon prepared mustard
  Salt and pepper to taste
- 6 slices bread, cubed
- 6 (1 oz.) slices process American cheese, slivered with sharp knife
- 2 green onions, cut fine (include some green tops)

In large mixing bowl combine eggs, wine, and water; beat just enough to blend. Add chicken stock base, Worcestershire sauce, mustard, salt, and pepper; stir in bread cubes, cheese slivers, and onions. Let stand an hour or so. Stir mixture well; pour into a 9-inch pie plate that has been greased with a tiny dab (⅛ teaspoon) of diet margarine. Bake in 325° oven 1 hour. Remove from oven; let stand 15 minutes before cutting. To serve, cut in 6 wedges with a sharp knife; ease wedges out gently with a spatula.

CHILI-CHEESE TART

(serves 6 / 220 calories per serving)

Follow recipe for Vineyard Cheese Tart (given). Remove seeds from all or part of 1 (4 oz.) can peeled green chili peppers; cut peppers fairly fine; add to bread-cheese mixture along with a generous pinch of oregano. No added calories to count, since peppers are an *all-you-want* vegetable.

PINEAPPLE COCKTAIL SALAD

(82 calories per serving)

For each serving, line a small salad plate with crisp salad greens *(all-you-want)*. On greens place a slice of juice-pack canned pineapple; top pineapple with ¼ cup well-drained calorie-reduced canned fruit cocktail. Over the fruit spoon 3 teaspoons (1 tablespoon) White Wine Dressing (page 79). Serve very cold.

JELLIED CHICKEN LOAF

(serves 8 / 184 calories per serving)

Place a whole (approximately 5 lb.) stewing chicken in a large kettle. Slice and add 1 carrot, 1 medium onion, 1 clove garlic, and 1 large stalk celery; add several sprigs parsley, 1 bay leaf, 2 whole cloves, 5 or 6 peppercorns, and 2 teaspoons salt. Pour in 1 cup California White Table Wine and enough boiling water so chicken is barely covered. Cover; simmer gently 2½ to 3 hours, or until chicken is fork-tender, turning chicken 2 or 3 times.

Let chicken cool in broth. Remove chicken; strain broth and chill so top layer of fat will be easier to remove. (To hasten the process, set container of broth in freezer briefly.) Remove skin from chicken; discard skin; separate meat from bones. Put meat through food grinder with 2 tender stalks celery and 2 green onions (including a little of the green tops). Remove layer of fat from broth. Measure broth; boil rapidly until reduced to 4 cups, or add water and chicken stock base (1 teaspoon base per cup of water) as needed to make 4 cups. For remainder of recipe proceed as follows:

- 2 envelopes unflavored gelatin
- ½ cup California White Table Wine
- 4 cups chicken broth (above)
- 1 tablespoon chopped chives or parsley
- 2 teaspoons lemon juice
- 2 teaspoons Worcestershire sauce
  Dash of Tabasco sauce or cayenne
  Seasoned salt and pepper to taste

Soften gelatin in the wine. Heat 1 cup chicken broth to boiling; add softened gelatin and stir until dissolved; add to remaining 3 cups broth. Stir in ground chicken, celery, and onion, mixing well. Add remaining ingredients. Taste and be sure the mixture has real "zip." Turn into a loaf pan (10 by 5 by 3 inches) that has been rinsed with cold water; chill until firm. Unmold on lettuce-lined platter. To serve, slice with very sharp knife. Serve with Egg Dressing (following). Dressing portion for this salad: 4 tablespoons / 48 calories.

BUFFET HALIBUT LOAF

(serves 8 / 214 calories per serving)

 3 cups water
 1 cup California White Table Wine
 ½ medium-sized onion, sliced
 1 clove garlic, sliced
 6 whole cloves
 1 bay leaf
5 or 6 whole peppercorns
   Salt to taste
 2 pounds halibut steaks
 1½ envelopes (1½ tablespoons) unflavored gelatin
 ¼ cup cold water
 1 cup plain low-fat yoghurt
 1 tablespoon California white wine vinegar
 1 tablespoon lemon juice
 2 tablespoons finely cut green onion
 1 teaspoon Worcestershire sauce
 ½ teaspoon Dijon prepared mustard
 ¼ teaspoon paprika
   Pepper to taste
 2 hard-cooked eggs, shredded or chopped
 ¾ cup finely cut celery
 1 (2¼ oz.) bottle capers, drained (⅓ cup)
 2 tablespoons chopped parsley

Combine the 3 cups water and the wine in a large skillet; add onion, garlic, cloves, bay leaf, peppercorns, and salt; bring to a boil. Lay fish steaks in this liquid; cover and simmer very gently about 10 minutes, or just until fish is tender. Drain fish, reserving liquid; flake fish, removing any skin and bones. Strain liquid; boil rapidly, uncovered, until reduced to 1½ cups. Soften gelatin in the ¼ cup cold water; dissolve in the hot fish liquid. Blend in yoghurt; add vinegar, lemon juice, green onion, Worcestershire sauce, prepared mustard, paprika, salt, and pepper. Chill until mixture begins to thicken, then fold in flaked fish and all remaining ingredients, mixing gently but thoroughly. Pour into a loaf pan (10 by 5 by 3 inches) that has been rinsed with cold water; press down with back of spoon to smooth surface. Chill until firm. Unmold on lettuce-lined platter. To serve, slice with very sharp knife. Serve with Cucumber Dressing (following). Dressing portion for this salad: 4 tablespoons / 24 calories.

EGG DRESSING

(12 calories per tablespoon)

 1½ cups plain low-fat yoghurt
 1½ tablespoons California Dry Vermouth
 1 teaspoon California white wine vinegar
 ¾ teaspoon yellow prepared mustard
 ¾ teaspoon Worcestershire sauce
 1½ teaspoons seasoned salt
 2 tablespoons each: chopped parsley and pimiento
 1 tablespoon finely cut green onion
 ½ clove garlic, chopped or pressed
 2 hard-cooked eggs, shredded or finely chopped

Blend yoghurt, wine, vinegar, mustard, Worcestershire sauce, and salt. Add remaining ingredients; mix well. Cover; chill several hours or overnight before serving. Makes 2 cups.

CUCUMBER DRESSING

(6 calories per tablespoon)

Follow recipe for Egg Dressing (given), but omit eggs and add ⅔ cup shredded or chopped seeded, peeled cucumber and a generous sprinkling of dill weed. (Drain cucumber by pressing between paper towels before adding to yoghurt mixture.) Makes 2⅓ cups.

SLICED TOMATOES WITH HERBS

(serves 8 / 28 calories per serving)

Peel 4 medium-sized tomatoes; cut each crosswise in 4 slices; arrange on a lettuce-lined platter. Crush 1 clove garlic with ½ teaspoon salt; stir in 3 tablespoons White Wine Dressing (page 79); add ¼ cup finely chopped parsley and 1 tablespoon chopped fresh basil or ½ teaspoon dried basil; mix well. Spread herb mixture on tomato slices; chill 1 hour or so before serving.

MENU 8

(1200 calories)

BREAKFAST
(200 calories)

Tomato Juice
*(¾ cup flavored with a sprinkling of dill weed and a generous squeeze of lemon juice /
35 calories)*

Scrambled Onion Egg
(1 egg beaten with 1 tablespoon water, bit of grated onion and dash of Worcestershire sauce; scramble in ungreased Teflon skillet / 80 calories)

Toast
(1 slice with 1 teaspoon diet margarine / 82 calories)

Black Coffee or Tea

LUNCH
(300 calories)

Chef's Special Salad Bowl*
or Chicken Luncheon Salad Bowl*
with
Tangy Dressing*

Black Coffee or Tea

DINNER
(550 calories)

Hot or Chilled Asparagus with Mustard Sauce*

Sole Monterey* or Sole with Mushrooms*
or Sole Athene*

Zucchini or Green Beans
(all-you-want vegetables)

Chive Baked Potato*
Brandy Broiled Grapefruit*

Wine Choice: California Grey Riesling

Extra Foods for Non-Slimmers:

Breakfast: Ham or crisp bacon

Lunch: Crescent rolls; fruit-flavored gelatin dessert with frozen whipped dessert topping

Dinner: Macaroons with the grapefruit

The 1200-calorie figure includes 100 calories for the 4-ounce glass of dry Table Wine and 50 calories for the *all-you-want* vegetables as listed on page 14 and used in the menus and recipes. Recipes are included for all dishes marked with an asterisk.

CHEF'S SPECIAL SALAD BOWL

(303 calories per serving)

For each serving allow:

- 2 cups bite-size pieces chilled salad greens
- 1 (1 oz.) slice process American cheese, slivered
- 1 (1 oz.) slice boiled ham, slivered
- ½ medium-sized tomato, cut in wedges
- ¼ hard-cooked egg, shredded
- ⅓ cup packaged herb-seasoned stuffing croutons
- 3 tablespoons Tangy Dressing (following)

Place greens in an individual salad bowl. Arrange cheese, ham, and tomato wedges over greens; sprinkle egg and croutons over top. Just before serving, add dressing; toss gently to mix ingredients.

CHICKEN LUNCHEON SALAD BOWL

(300 calories per serving)

For each serving allow:

- 2 cups bite-size chilled salad greens
- ½ cup thinly sliced raw, cooked, or canned mushrooms
- 1 green onion, thinly sliced (include a little of the green top)
- 2 ounces slivered, cooked white meat of chicken (approx. ½ cup)
- ½ (1 oz.) slice process Swiss cheese, slivered
- ¼ hard-cooked egg, shredded
- ¼ cup packaged herb-seasoned stuffing croutons
- 3 tablespoons Tangy Dressing (following)

Place greens in an individual salad bowl; add mushrooms and onion; mix gently. Arrange chicken and cheese slivers over greens; top with egg and croutons. Just before serving, add dressing; toss gently to mix ingredients.

TANGY DRESSING

(7 calories per teaspoon, 21 per tablespoon)

- ½ cup vegetable juice cocktail
- ¼ cup California Dry Vermouth
- 2 tablespoons California white wine tarragon vinegar
- 2 tablespoons vegetable salad oil
- 1 clove garlic, chopped or pressed
- 1 teaspoon salt
- ½ teaspoon Worcestershire sauce
- ¼ teaspoon each: coarse ground pepper, paprika, and dry mustard

Combine all ingredients in a jar or bowl; shake or beat to mix well. Chill, covered, for at least an hour to blend flavors. Always shake or beat well before serving. Makes 1 cup. Fine with mixed green, vegetable, and many fruit salads.

ASPARAGUS WITH MUSTARD SAUCE

(41 calories per serving, including sauce)

For each serving, allow 6 spears hot or chilled cooked or canned asparagus and 2 tablespoons Mustard Sauce (following). Arrange asparagus on plate; spoon sauce over; dust with paprika. A few little frilly lettuce leaves make a good *all-you-want* garnish for the cold asparagus, parsley sprigs for the hot.

Mustard Sauce: Blend ½ cup plain low-fat yoghurt, 1 teaspoon prepared mustard (the yellow variety), and ½ teaspoon each California Dry Vermouth and lemon juice. Season with a generous sprinkling of lemon pepper and salt to taste. Makes ½ cup / 8 calories per tablespoon.

SOLE MONTEREY

(serves 3 / 312 calories per serving)

Fold 1 pound fillets of sole so shiny skin side is inside; place in single layer in shallow baking dish. Over fillets pour ¾ cup California White Table Wine and ½ cup water; add 2 thin slices onion, 1 bay leaf, 3 or 4 whole peppercorns, dash of thyme, and ½ teaspoon salt. Cover dish loosely with aluminum foil; bake in 350° oven 15 minutes. Remove fillets from liquid; gently pat dry with paper towels. Discard liquid; put fillets back in dish. For remainder of recipe proceed as follows:

> ½ cup undiluted evaporated skim milk
> ½ cup cold water
> 2 tablespoons instant-blending flour
> 1 teaspoon chicken stock base
> 1 tablespoon diet margarine
> 1 tablespoon Dijon prepared mustard
> 1 tablespoon California Dry Sherry
> ¼ teaspoon Worcestershire sauce
> Salt, garlic salt, and pepper to taste
> 1 tablespoon each: chopped chives and parsley
> 2 tablespoons grated Parmesan cheese
> Paprika

In small saucepan combine evaporated milk, water, flour, chicken stock base, and margarine; stir over medium heat until mixture boils and thickens. Blend in mustard and Sherry; add remaining ingredients except cheese and paprika. Spoon hot sauce over fillets in baking dish; sprinkle with cheese. Bake, uncovered, in 350° oven 10 minutes; place under broiler briefly to brown top. Remove from oven; dust with paprika; let rest 5 minutes or so before serving.

SOLE WITH MUSHROOMS

(serves 3 / 315 calories per serving)

Poach 1 pound folded fillets of sole in the oven as directed above for Sole Monterey, but scatter ½ pound thinly sliced fresh mushrooms over the fish before pouring liquids over it. At end of poaching period, remove sole and mushrooms from dish, reserving liquid. Strain liquid; boil rapidly until reduced to ½ cup. Pat fish dry with paper towels; replace mushrooms in baking dish. For remainder of recipe proceed as follows:

> ½ cup undiluted evaporated skim milk
> ½ cup reduced fish stock (above)
> 2 tablespoons instant-blending flour
> 1 tablespoon diet margarine
> 2 tablespoons California Dry Sherry
> ¼ teaspoon grated lemon peel
> ¼ teaspoon Worcestershire sauce
> Seasoned salt and pepper to taste
> 1 tablespoon each: chopped chives and parsley
> 3 tablespoons grated Parmesan cheese
> Paprika

In small saucepan combine evaporated milk, fish stock, flour, and margarine; stir over medium heat until mixture boils and thickens. Add all remaining ingredients except cheese and paprika. Spoon hot sauce over sole and mushrooms; sprinkle with cheese. Bake, uncovered, in 350° oven 10 minutes; place under broiler briefly to brown top. Remove from oven; dust with paprika; let rest 5 minutes or so before serving.

SOLE ATHENE

(serves 3 / 317 calories per serving)

Follow recipe for Baked Sole with Mushrooms (given), but reduce Parmesan cheese to 1 tablespoon; add ½ cup fresh (or drained water-pack canned) seedless grapes to the hot sauce before pouring it over the fish and mushrooms.

Lacking fresh or water-pack canned grapes, you can use syrup-pack canned grapes. Drain them thoroughly in a strainer, then rinse under running water.

CHIVE BAKED POTATO

(118 calories per serving)

Allow 1 medium (3-to-a-lb.) potato, 1½ teaspoons diet margarine, and 1 teaspoon chopped chives per serving. Scrub and bake the potato as usual. (In a 350° oven with the fish, it will need about 1 hour and 10 minutes.) Melt margarine in a small saucepan; add chives. Split open potato; fluff with a fork; pour in sauce. Add salt and pepper to taste. Eat and enjoy, but omit the skin for this calorie count.

BRANDY BROILED GRAPEFRUIT

(78 calories per serving)

For each serving, allow ½ grapefruit, 1 tablespoon California Brandy, and 1 teaspoon brown sugar. Place grapefruit halves in shallow baking dish; loosen pulp from peel with a grapefruit knife. Spoon Brandy over fruit; sprinkle with brown sugar. Broil, about 4 inches from source of heat, until bubbly and delicately browned. Watch carefully; baste with any juices that may escape during broiling.

MENU

9

(1200 calories)

BREAKFAST
(200 calories)

Sliced Orange
(1 medium orange / 60 calories)

Caraway Cheese
(⅓ cup low-fat cottage cheese seasoned with dry shredded green onion or chopped chives and a sprinkling of caraway seeds / 67 calories)

Rye Toast
(1 slice with ½ teaspoon diet margarine / 74 calories)

Black Coffee or Tea

LUNCH
(300 calories)

Hot Luncheon Sandwich Poulet*
Mixed Green Salad with Italian Herb Dressing*
Black Coffee or Tea

DINNER
(550 calories)

Shrimp and Cucumber Cocktail*

Broiled or Barbecued Flank Steak,*
Steak Strips,* or Steak-Mushroom Roll-Ups*
or
Savory Pork Skewers*

Bean Sprouts
(fresh or canned sprouts, all-you-want, seasoned with a sprinkling of soy sauce)

Peas with Celery
(the frozen combination, ½ cup / 58 calories)

Peach Perfection*

Wine Choice: California Gamay

Extra Foods for Non-Slimmers:

Breakfast: Thin slices of bologna or chipped beef

Lunch: Slice of process American or Swiss cheese on the toast on top of the chicken spread; date bar or brownie for dessert

Dinner: Frozen French-fried or hash brown potatoes; trickle of California Sweet Sherry over the dessert topping

The 1200-calorie figure includes 100 calories for the 4-ounce glass of dry Table Wine and 50 calories for the *all-you-want* vegetables as listed on page 14 and used in the menus and recipes. Recipes are included for all dishes marked with an asterisk.

HOT LUNCHEON SANDWICH POULET

(serves 3 / 251 calories per serving)

  1 (4 oz.) can sliced mushrooms
  ½ cup evaporated skim milk
  2 tablespoons instant-blending flour
  1 teaspoon chicken stock base
  1 tablespoon diet margarine
  3 tablespoons California White Table Wine
  1 tablespoon California Dry Sherry
  2 tablespoons chopped parsley
  ¼ teaspoon each: Worcestershire sauce and
     grated lemon peel
     Seasoned salt and pepper to taste
  3 slices hot, crisp toast
  1 (4¾ oz.) can chicken spread
  1 (10 oz.) package frozen broccoli or
     asparagus spears, cooked and drained
  3 tablespoons grated Parmesan cheese
     Paprika

Drain mushrooms, reserving liquid. In a saucepan combine mushroom liquid and milk; add flour, chicken stock base, and margarine; cook, stirring, over medium heat until mixture boils and thickens. Add white wine, Sherry, parsley, and seasonings; stir in mushrooms.

To assemble sandwich: Spread each slice of toast with some of the chicken spread; arrange hot broccoli or asparagus spears on top; spoon sauce over all. Sprinkle with Parmesan cheese; dust with paprika. Serve at once.

MIXED GREEN SALAD, ITALIAN HERB DRESSING

(48 calories per serving, including dressing)

Choose whatever combination of chilled, crisp greens you like, not forgetting tender leaves of watercress, if available. Add thinly sliced radishes and green pepper slivers, if you like. (Greens, radishes, and green pepper are *all-you-want* ingredients.) Toss all together with Italian Herb Dressing (following) allowing 2 tablespoons dressing per portion.

ITALIAN HERB DRESSING

(8 calories per teaspoon; 24 per tablespoon)

  ½ cup California White Table Wine
  2 tablespoons California white wine
     tarragon vinegar
  2 tablespoons vegetable salad oil
  2 tablespoons chopped parsley
  1 tablespoon chopped pimiento
  1 clove garlic, chopped or pressed
  ½ teaspoon Worcestershire sauce
  ¾ teaspoon salt
  ¼ teaspoon each: coarse pepper, rosemary,
     oregano, and basil

Combine all ingredients in a jar or bowl; shake or beat to mix well. Chill, covered, for at least an hour to blend flavors. Always shake or beat well before using. Makes 1 cup. Excellent with green, vegetable, and many seafood salads.

SHRIMP AND CUCUMBER COCKTAIL

(serves 4 / 80 calories per serving)

  1 (4½ oz.) can small shrimp, drained
     (approx. 1 cup)
  ½ cup finely diced, peeled, seeded
     cucumber
  ¼ cup each: catsup and chili sauce
  2 tablespoons California Dry Vermouth
  1½ teaspoons lemon juice
  ½ teaspoon grated onion
  1 teaspoon prepared horseradish
  ¼ teaspoon Worcestershire sauce
     Dash of Tabasco sauce
     Salt to taste

Mix shrimp and cucumber; cover; chill an hour or more. Mix remaining ingredients; chill. At serving time, spoon shrimp and cucumber into lettuce-lined cocktail cups or onto small lettuce-lined plates; top with the sauce. Pass lemon wedges (no added calories).

Diced heart of celery is very good here in place of the cucumber. (Calories remain the same.)

BROILED OR BARBECUED FLANK STEAK

(serves 4 / 303 calories per serving)

1 flank steak (about 1½ lbs.), not
   tenderized
¼ cup California Red Table Wine
2 tablespoons soy sauce
½ clove garlic, chopped or pressed
1 teaspoon finely grated onion
⅛ teaspoon each: thyme, marjoram,
   rosemary, and coarse pepper

With tip of a sharp knife, score steak on both sides in 1½-inch diamonds; place in a shallow glass dish. Mix remaining ingredients; pour over steak; turn steak over in mixture 2 or 3 times so it's well coated. Cover dish with aluminum foil or transparent wrap; let steak marinate in refrigerator several hours; turn occasionally. Remove from refrigerator an hour or so before cooking so meat will be at room temperature. Broil 3 to 4 inches from heat, 5 minutes to a side. (No more!) Or, grill 5 minutes to a side on the barbecue. To serve, slice thinly on diagonal across grain.

BROILED OR BARBECUED STEAK STRIPS

(serves 4 / 303 calories per serving)

Buy a 1½-pound flank steak; do not have it tenderized. Using a meat tenderizer or a mallet, pound steak to flatten thick part. Cut steak diagonally across grain into 8 strips; pound strips as necessary to make them more uniform in length. Prepare wine marinade as directed above for Barbecued Flank Steak; marinate strips several hours or overnight, turning occasionally. Broil or barbecue, allowing only about 2 minutes per side.

STEAK-MUSHROOM ROLL-UPS

(serves 4 / 303 calories per serving)

Prepare 8 steak strips as directed above for Broiled or Barbecued Steak Strips. With a damp sponge or cloth, wipe 8 fresh mushrooms (about 2 inches in diameter); cut off stems flush with caps. Encircle each mushroom with a steak strip; fasten strips with skewers or tie with cord. Place, with cut side of mushroom down, in a single layer in a shallow dish. Prepare wine marinade as directed above for Broiled or Barbecued Flank Steak; spoon over roll-ups. Cover; marinate several hours or overnight, spooning marinade over roll-ups occasionally. Broil or barbecue, allowing 5 minutes per side. Calorie count remains the same, since mushrooms are an *all-you-want* vegetable.

SAVORY PORK SKEWERS

(serves 4 / 305 calories per serving)

1¼ pounds boneless loin of pork, cut in
   1-inch cubes
¼ cup California Rosé
¼ cup soy sauce
1 tablespoon brown sugar
1 clove garlic, chopped or pressed
½ teaspoon grated fresh ginger root, or ¼
   teaspoon powdered ginger

Place pork in single layer in shallow glass dish. Mix remaining ingredients; pour over pork, stirring to coat meat. Cover dish with foil or transparent wrap; let meat marinate in refrigerator several hours; stir occasionally. An hour or so before cooking, remove from refrigerator; thread meat cubes on 8 (5- to 6-inch) skewers; place on rack in a shallow baking pan. Bake in 300° oven 1 hour, basting several times with the marinade.

PEACH PERFECTION

(serves 5 / 96 calories per serving)

½ cup California Sweet Sherry
¼ cup cold water
1 envelope unflavored gelatin
¼ cup sugar
   Dash of salt
1 cup orange juice
1 cup diced, drained calorie-reduced
   canned peaches
¼ teaspoon almond extract

Combine wine and water in a small saucepan; sprinkle in gelatin; stir over low heat 2 to 3 minutes, until gelatin is completely dissolved. Stir in sugar and salt; add orange juice. Pour about ⅓ of this liquid into blender container; add ⅓ of the peaches; blend several minutes, until peaches are completely liquified; pour into a bowl. Repeat process twice more with remaining liquid and peaches, ⅓ at a time. Stir in almond extract. Pour into 5 sherbet glasses or dessert dishes; chill until firm, stirring gently 2 or 3 times at first to prevent separation. At serving time, top each portion with 1 tablespoon frozen whipped dessert topping (16 calories).

MENU

10

(1200 calories)

BREAKFAST
(200 calories)

Strawberries
(1 cup capped fresh or unsweetened frozen berries / 53 calories)

Hot or Dry Cereal
(¾ cup instant or quick-cooking hot cereal, or 1 cup rice, corn, or wheat flakes; ½ cup non-fat milk; non-caloric sweetener, if desired / 144 calories)

Black Coffee or Tea

LUNCH
(300 calories)

Salad Plate:

Tomato-Artichoke Aspic* with Shrimp or Crabmeat and Green Chili Dressing*
or
Seafood Aspic Molds with Tomatoes and Artichoke Hearts* and Caper-Cheese Dressing or Anchovy-Tarragon Dressing

Parmesan Muffin
(½ lightly toasted English muffin spread with 1 teaspoon diet margarine, then sprinkled with 1 teaspoon grated Parmesan cheese and paprika; broil briefly to melt cheese; cut in halves / 99 calories)

Peaches
(½ cup sliced fresh or calorie-reduced canned peaches / 33 calories)

Black Coffee or Tea

DINNER
(550 calories)

Lemony Beet Salad*

Breast of Chicken with Grapes*

Broccoli
(2 small spears or ½ cup chopped broccoli, topped with 1 teaspoon grated Parmesan cheese and dusting of paprika / 33 calories)

Rice
(½ cup cooked long-grain white rice / 91 calories)

Pumpkin Custard*

Wine Choice: California Pinot Chardonnay

Extra Foods for Non-Slimmers:

Breakfast: Sweet roll

Lunch: Slices of avocado added to the salad; vanilla wafers with the peaches

Dinner: Vanilla ice milk on the Pumpkin Custard

The 1200-calorie figure includes 100 calories for the 4-ounce glass of dry Table Wine and 50 calories for the *all-you-want* vegetables as listed on page 14 and used in the menus and recipes. Recipes are included for all dishes marked with an asterisk.

TOMATO-ARTICHOKE ASPIC

(serves 5 / 46 calories per serving)

  1½ envelopes (1 tablespoon plus 1½
       teaspoons) unflavored gelatin
   ¼ cup California White Table Wine
    2 cups canned tomato juice
   ½ cup canned condensed bouillon (beef
       broth)
  1½ teaspoons California white wine
       tarragon vinegar
3 or 4 celery leaves
   ½ bay leaf
    3 whole peppercorns
    2 whole cloves
    1 thick slice onion
    1 teaspoon sugar
   ½ teaspoon Worcestershire sauce
       Salt to taste
    5 canned (not marinated) artichoke
       hearts, rinsed and drained

Soften gelatin in the wine. Combine tomato juice in saucepan with all remaining ingredients except salt and artichoke hearts; bring to boil; cover and simmer 10 minutes; strain. Add softened gelatin to hot liquid; stir until dissolved. Season with salt to taste. Chill mixture until the consistency of unbeaten egg white.

Meantime, cut artichoke hearts lengthwise in thirds (or quarters, if large); divide hearts among 5 individual molds or 6-ounce custard cups that have been rinsed with cold water. Spoon partially thickened tomato mixture over artichokes; chill until firm. At serving time, unmold on crisp salad greens (*all-you-want*).

To complete Salad Plate: Surround molds with cooked or canned shrimp (½ cup per portion) or flaked crabmeat (⅓ cup per portion). Serve with Green Chili Dressing (following). Dressing portion for this salad: 4 tablespoons. Total calories for the Salad Plate: 165.

GREEN CHILI DRESSING

(11 calories per tablespoon)

    1 cup low-fat cottage cheese
    2 tablespoons cultured buttermilk
  1½ teaspoons California Dry Vermouth
  1½ teaspoons California white wine vinegar
   ½ teaspoon salt
   ¼ teaspoon garlic salt
   ¼ teaspoon Worcestershire sauce
    2 tablespoons chopped, seeded canned
       green chili peppers
   ¼ cup (firmly packed) parsley sprigs
       (no stems)
    1 tablespoon chopped onion

Combine all ingredients in blender; whirl until smooth. Cover; chill at least an hour to blend flavors. Makes 1⅓ cups.

This dressing has a lovely green color and a decided nip that makes it especially good with tomatoes. It also makes a perfect dip for raw cauliflowerets, celery sticks, etc., as does Pimiento Cream Dressing (page 61). For a less spicy flavor, decrease the amount of chili pepper, or substitute fresh green pepper. No change in the calorie count.

SEA FOOD ASPIC MOLDS WITH TOMATOES AND ARTICHOKE HEARTS

(serves 8 / 125 calories per serving)

    2 envelopes unflavored gelatin
   ½ cup California Dry Vermouth
  1⅓ cups canned chicken broth (not
       condensed)
    1 (8 oz.) bottle clam juice
    1 tablespoon California white wine
       vinegar
    1 tablespoon lemon juice
    1 teaspoon grated onion
    1 teaspoon Worcestershire sauce
       Salt and pepper to taste
    2 cups small fresh shrimp, or 2 (4½ oz.)
       cans
    1 cup flaked fresh crabmeat, or 1 (7½ oz.)
       can
    3 tablespoons chopped parsley
    4 medium-sized tomatoes, peeled and cut
       in sixths
    1 (9 oz.) package frozen artichoke hearts,
       cooked and drained

Sprinkle gelatin over wine in small saucepan; stir over low heat about 3 minutes, until gelatin is dissolved. Remove from heat. Combine gelatin mixture with chicken broth, clam juice, vinegar, lemon juice, onion, and seasonings; blend well. Chill until mixture is consistency of unbeaten egg white.

With fork, gently mix shrimp, crabmeat, and parsley; divide evenly among 8 (6-ounce) custard cups that have been rinsed with cold water (about ⅓ cup seafood mixture per custard cup); spoon slightly thickened gelatin mixture over seafood. Chill until firm. At serving time, unmold on crisp salad greens (*all-you-want*).

To complete Salad Plate: Arrange 3 tomato wedges and some of the artichoke hearts around each mold. Serve with Caper Cheese Dressing (page 91) or Anchovy Tarragon Dressing (page 94). Dressing portion for this salad: 4 tablespoons. Total calories for the Salad Plate: 169.

LEMONY BEET SALAD

(serves 8 / 51 calories per serving)

2 (1 lb.) cans julienne beets
Grated peel of 1 lemon
¼ cup lemon juice
¼ cup California Red Table Wine
2 tablespoons California red wine vinegar
2 tablespoons brown sugar
1 teaspoon salt
Freshly ground pepper to taste

Drain beets thoroughly; place in quart jar or bowl. Stir remaining ingredients together; pour over beets. Cover jar or bowl; refrigerate at least 24 hours before serving. Turn jar occasionally; or, if beets are in a bowl, stir gently from time to time.

At serving time, line salad plates with crisp greens *(all-you-want)*; place drained beets (½ cup per portion) on greens.

BREAST OF CHICKEN WITH GRAPES

(serves 6 / 259 calories per serving)

2 tablespoons diet margarine
3 (approx. 10 oz.) whole chicken breasts, boned and halved
Salt, pepper, paprika, and thyme
¾ cup canned chicken broth (not condensed)
½ cup California White Table Wine
2 tablespoons each: chopped green onion and chopped parsley
1 clove garlic, chopped or pressed
1 (4 oz.) can sliced mushrooms, drained (reserve liquid)
2 tablespoons instant-blending flour
½ cup undiluted evaporated skim milk
1 tablespoon California Medium Sherry
½ teaspoon Worcestershire sauce
Dash of nutmeg
¾ cup fresh or water-pack canned seedless grapes (or well-rinsed syrup-pack canned grapes)

Melt margarine in large Teflon skillet; place chicken in pan, skin side down; sauté slowly until golden brown. Turn chicken skin side up; sprinkle with salt, pepper, paprika, and thyme; continue sautéing until browned on the underside. Add chicken broth, white wine, onion, parsley, and garlic; cover; simmer very gently 30 minutes or so, until chicken is tender, turning pieces occasionally.

Remove chicken from skillet; set aside. Pour broth into measuring pitcher; skim off fat; add enough reserved mushroom liquid (and water if needed) to make 1½ cups; pour back into skillet. Blend flour with evaporated milk; add to broth in skillet; stir over medium heat until mixture boils and thickens. Add Sherry, Worcestershire sauce, nutmeg, grapes, and mushrooms; season to taste with salt and pepper. Return chicken to skillet; cover; heat gently but thoroughly before serving.

If you want to make this dish early in the day, return chicken to sauce in skillet as directed; let cool, then cover and refrigerate. Reheat gently before serving. The flavor will be all the better for this mellowing period.

PUMPKIN CUSTARD

(serves 6 / 97 calories per serving)

¾ cup undiluted evaporated skim milk
½ cup water
¼ cup California Medium Sherry
1 cup canned pumpkin
6 tablespoons sugar
¼ teaspoon each: cinnamon and nutmeg
Dash of cloves
¼ teaspoon salt
4 egg whites

In mixing bowl, combine milk, water, and Sherry; blend in pumpkin; add sugar, spices, and salt. Beat egg whites with fork just until well mixed and slightly foamy; blend into pumpkin mixture. Pour into 6 custard cups; set in shallow pan; pour in boiling water to depth of 1 inch. Bake in 350° oven about 35 minutes, or until knife inserted near center comes out clean. Remove cups to wire rack to cool; chill before serving. Top each portion with 1 tablespoon frozen whipped dessert topping (16 calories).

MENU
11

(1200 calories)

BREAKFAST
(200 calories)

Grapefruit
(½ medium grapefruit / 55 calories)

Scrambled Egg with Croutons
*(mix 1 egg with 1 tablespoon water, a sprinkling
of dry shredded green onions, and seasonings to
taste; scramble in ungreased Teflon pan; serve
topped with ⅓ cup herb-seasoned stuffing croutons
and 1 tablespoon grated Parmesan cheese /
140 calories)*

Black Coffee or Tea

LUNCH
(300 calories)

Stuffed Zucchini Venetia*
or
**Chicken-Mushroom Stuffed Zucchini
with Tomato Sauce***

Crisp Radishes and Celery Hearts
(all you want)

Toast or Golden Toast Strips
*(1 slice toast with 1 teaspoon diet margarine,
or 4 Strips, page 28 / 84 calories)*

Black Coffee or Tea

DINNER
(550 calories)

**Orange and Cucumber Salad
with Green Onion Dressing***

Scallops Jacqueline*
or
Scallops Sauté*
with Yoghurt Tartar Sauce or Caper Sauce

Green Beans
(all-you-want)

Baked Potato
*(1 medium, 3-to-a-lb., with 1 tablespoon
diet margarine; omit skin / 143 calories)*

Brandied Coffee Strata*

Wine Choice: California Dry Sauterne

Extra Foods for Non-Slimmers:

Breakfast: Canadian bacon

Lunch: Canned shoestring potatoes; frozen butterscotch pudding for dessert

Dinner: Whole-kernel corn added to the green beans;
a trickle of California Brandy over the dessert
topping

The 1200-calorie figure includes 100 calories for the 4-ounce glass of dry Table Wine and 50 calories for the *all-you-want* vegetable as
listed on page 14 and used in the menus and recipes. Recipes are included for all dishes marked with an asterisk.

CHICKEN-MUSHROOM STUFFED ZUCCHINI WITH TOMATO SAUCE

(serves 4 / 215 calories per serving, including sauce and cheese)

  4 zucchini, about 6 inches long (approx. 1 lb.)
  1 (4¾ oz.) can chicken spread
  1 (4 oz.) can mushroom stems and pieces, drained and finely chopped
  2 tablespoons grated Parmesan cheese
  1 tablespoon California Medium Sherry
  2 tablespoons chopped parsley
  1 tablespoon chopped green onion
  ½ teaspoon Worcestershire sauce
    Dash of thyme
    Seasoned salt and pepper to taste
  6 (¾ oz.) slices process American cheese

Cook zucchini and prepare shells as directed in the recipe for Stuffed Zucchini Venetia (given). Chop scooped out portion fine; drain; combine with all remaining ingredients except sliced cheese. Sprinkle zucchini shells with salt; fill with chicken-mushroom mixture; place in shallow baking pan. Cut each cheese slice in 4 strips; drape 3 over each zucchini half. Bake in 350° oven about 20 minutes, or until cheese melts. Serve with Tomato Sauce (following) and Parmesan cheese. Sauce portion is ¼ cup; cheese, 2 teaspoons.

TOMATO SAUCE

(1 cup / 87 calories)

In a saucepan combine 1 (8 oz.) can tomato sauce, ¼ cup California White Table Wine, 1 teaspoon grated onion, bit of chopped or pressed garlic, ¼ teaspoon sugar, ⅛ teaspoon mixed Italian seasoning, and salt and pepper to taste. Cover; simmer 10 minutes, stirring frequently.

STUFFED ZUCCHINI VENETIA

(serves 4 / 218 calories per serving)

  4 zucchini, about 6 inches long (approx. 1 lb.)
  1 (10 oz.) package frozen chopped spinach, cooked and thoroughly drained
  1 cup finely diced, cooked chicken
  1 tablespoon finely chopped green onion
  ¼ cup undiluted evaporated skim milk
  ¼ cup water
  2 tablespoons instant-blending flour
  ½ teaspoon chicken stock base
  1 tablespoon California Medium Sherry
    Pinch each of rosemary and oregano
    Seasoned salt and pepper to taste
  4 (1 oz.) slices process American cheese
    Chopped parsley or paprika

Wash zucchini and trim off ends; cook whole in boiling salted water about 10 minutes, or just until tender; drain. When cool enough to handle, cut lengthwise in halves and scoop out insides. Turn shells upside down on paper towels to drain. Chop scooped out portion fine; drain; combine with spinach, chicken, and onion. In a small saucepan, mix milk and water; blend in flour and chicken stock base; cook, stirring, over medium heat until sauce boils and thickens. Remove from heat; add Sherry. Combine this sauce with spinach mixture; add herbs, salt, and pepper. Fill zucchini shells with the mixture; place in shallow baking pan. Cut each cheese slice in 4 strips; drape 2 over each zucchini half. Bake in 350° oven about 20 minutes, or until cheese melts. Before serving, sprinkle with chopped parsley or paprika.

ORANGE AND CUCUMBER SALAD, GREEN ONION DRESSING

(96 calories per serving, including dressing)

For each person allow 1 medium orange; peel and slice. Arrange slices on crisp romaine or other lettuce, alternately with slices of cucumber *(all-you-want)*. Chill salad thoroughly. Just before serving, spoon Green Onion Dressing (page 25) over the salad. Dressing portion: 4 teaspoons.

SCALLOPS JACQUELINE

(serves 3 / 223 calories per serving)

1 (4 oz.) can sliced mushrooms
½ cup California Dry Vermouth
¼ cup water
   Salt
1 bay leaf
1 pound scallops (thawed if frozen)
1 tablespoon finely chopped onion
2 teaspoons diet margarine
3 tablespoons instant-blending flour
¾ cup undiluted evaporated skim milk
   Dash of thyme
   Pepper to taste
2 tablespoons chopped parsley
1 tablespoon grated Parmesan cheese
   Paprika

Drain mushrooms, reserving liquid. In saucepan combine mushroom liquid, wine, water, dash of salt, and bay leaf; heat to simmering. Add scallops; cover; simmer 5 minutes. Remove scallops from liquid; boil liquid rapidly until reduced to ¾ cup. If scallops are large, cut in halves or quarters. Sauté onion gently in margarine 5 minutes. Blend flour and milk; stir in reduced scallop liquid; add to onion and cook, stirring constantly, over medium heat until mixture comes to boil. Season with thyme, salt, and pepper; add parsley. Divide scallops and mushrooms among 3 baking shells or individual casseroles; spoon sauce over them; sprinkle with cheese and paprika. Bake in 400° oven 10 minutes.

SCALLOPS SAUTÉ

*(serves 3 / 221 calories per serving,
including sauce)*

1 pound scallops (thawed if frozen)
¾ cup California White Table Wine
2 tablespoons flour
2 tablespoons diet margarine
   Seasoned salt and pepper to taste
1 lemon, cut in sixths
   Yogurt Tartar Sauce (page 26) or Caper
   Sauce (page 26).

If scallops are large, cut in halves or quarters. Place scallops in a single layer in a shallow dish; pour wine over them; let stand 30 minutes or so. Drain scallops, reserving ¼ cup wine; pat scallops dry with paper towels. Spread flour in a pie plate; add scallops, a few at a time; shake plate gently to coat scallops on all sides with flour. Melt margarine in a 10-inch Teflon skillet; place scallops in pan in a single layer; sauté over medium to medium-high heat for 4 or 5 minutes, shaking pan gently and turning scallops frequently to brown them on all sides. Add reserved ¼ cup wine; sprinkle with salt and pepper; cover and cook gently another minute. Serve immediately on heated dinner plates, accompanied by wedges of lemon. Pass Yoghurt Tartar Sauce or Caper Sauce. Sauce portion for this dish: 4 tablespoons.

BRANDIED COFFEE STRATA

(serves 4 / 84 calories per serving)

1½ cups cold water
¼ cup California Brandy
1 envelope unflavored gelatin
2 tablespoons instant coffee powder
¼ cup sugar
⅛ teaspoon salt

Combine ½ cup water and Brandy in a saucepan; sprinkle in gelatin; stir over low heat about 3 minutes, until gelatin is completely dissolved. Stir in coffee powder, sugar, and salt. Remove from heat; stir in remaining 1 cup cold water. Measure 1 cup gelatin mixture; pour into a bowl; chill until mixture mounds slightly when dropped from tip of a spoon. Pour remaining gelatin mixture into 4 sherbet glasses or dessert dishes; chill until almost firm. Beat thickened 1 cup gelatin mixture until doubled in volume; spoon over first layer; chill until firm. Before serving, top each portion with 1 tablespoon frozen whipped dessert topping (16 calories).

You can hasten the chilling of both parts of the gelatin mixture by setting them in the freezer, but watch carefully and don't let them get too firm.

BREAKFAST
(200 calories)

Cantaloupe
(½ small melon / 50 calories)

Deviled Mushroom Toast
(spread 1 slice toast with 1 tablespoon deviled ham; cover with sliced raw, briefly simmered, or canned mushrooms; sprinkle with 1½ tablespoons grated Parmesan cheese; bake or broil to heat / 148 calories)

Black Coffee or Tea

LUNCH
(300 calories)

Vegetable-Cottage Cheese Salad Plate*
with
Giovanni's Salad Dressing*
or
Mixed Green-Cottage Cheese Salad Bowl*
and
Giovanni's Tomato or Beet Salad*

Toasted English Muffin
(½ muffin with 1 teaspoon diet margarine / 90 calories)

Apricots
(2 fresh or canned calorie-reduced apricots / 38 calories)

Black Coffee or Tea

DINNER
(550 calories)

Tomato-Cucumber Cocktail*

Savory Pot Roast*

Zucchini and Mushrooms Sauté*

Hominy Grits or Cornmeal
(²/₃ cup cooked grits or cornmeal / 82 calories)

Cheesecake Tart*

Wine Choice: California Claret

Extra Foods for Non-Slimmers:

Breakfast: Top Deviled Mushroom Toast with a slice of process American cheese before baking or broiling

Lunch: Marinated artichoke hearts; creme-filled chocolate cookies with the apricots

Dinner: Parmesan cheese stirred into grits or cornmeal; spoonful of canned cherry or blueberry pie filling and/or dollop of sour half and half on Cheesecake Tart

The 1200-calorie figure includes 100 calories for the 4-ounce glass of dry Table Wine and 50 calories for the *all-you-want* vegetables as listed on page 14 and used in the menus and recipes. Recipes are included for all dishes marked with an asterisk.

VEGETABLE-COTTAGE CHEESE SALAD PLATE

(172 calories per serving, including dressing)

For each serving, line a luncheon plate with chilled, crisp salad greens. In the center place ½ cup low-fat cottage cheese mixed with 1 teaspoon or more chopped chives. Around the cheese arrange ½ medium tomato, sliced or cut in wedges; 2 canned (not marinated) or cooked frozen artichoke hearts, halved; a "bouquet" of briefly cooked cauliflowerets (an *all-you-want* vegetable). Crisscross 2 well-drained anchovy fillets over the cauliflower. Serve with Giovanni's Salad Dressing (following). Dressing portion for this salad: 2 tablespoons.

MIXED GREEN-COTTAGE CHEESE SALAD BOWL

(116 calories per serving)

For each serving, combine ½ cup low-fat cottage cheese and 2 tablespoons plain, low-fat yoghurt in an individual salad bowl. Stir in 1 chopped green onion, ½ teaspoon prepared horseradish, ½ teaspoon California white wine vinegar, a few drops of Worcestershire sauce, and seasoned salt and coarse pepper to taste. To this mixture add 2 cups bite-size pieces of crisp salad greens; toss lightly; serve at once.

GIOVANNI'S TOMATO OR BEET SALAD

(53 calories per serving, including dressing)

For each serving, allow 1 medium tomato, sliced, or ½ cup sliced cooked or canned beets. Lay slices in a shallow dish; spoon 4 teaspoons Giovanni's Salad Dressing (following) over them; chill an hour or so before serving on lettuce-lined salad plate.

GIOVANNI'S SALAD DRESSING

(5 calories per teaspoon, 15 per tablespoon)

- ½ cup tomato juice
- ¼ cup California Dry Vermouth
- 2 tablespoons California white wine vinegar
- 2 tablespoons vegetable salad oil
- 2 tablespoons each: very finely minced raw carrot, celery, onion, and parsley
- 1 clove garlic, chopped or pressed
- 1 teaspoon seasoned salt
- ½ teaspoon Worcestershire sauce
- ¼ teaspoon each: coarse pepper, paprika, and dry mustard

Combine all ingredients in a jar or bowl; shake or beat to mix well. Chill, covered, for at least an hour to blend flavors. Always shake or beat well before serving. Makes about 1½ cups. A very delicious dressing for mixed green and vegetable salads. Good with seafood, too.

TOMATO-CUCUMBER COCKTAIL

(serves 8 / 26 calories per serving)

- 4 cups (1 qt.) canned tomato juice
- ⅔ cup grated cucumber
- ½ teaspoon Worcestershire sauce
- 2 teaspoons sugar
- 2 teaspoons salt
- ¼ cup lemon juice
- 2 teaspoons prepared horseradish

Combine all ingredients; heat to simmering. Remove from heat; cool, then chill. At serving time, strain into juice glasses. Very refreshing. Leftover cocktail will keep its good flavor for several days if stored, covered, in the refrigerator.

ZUCCHINI AND MUSHROOMS SAUTÉ

(serves 6 to 8 / too few calories to count since these are all-you-want vegetables)

   2 pounds small zucchini
   1 pound fresh mushrooms
   ¼ cup California Dry Vermouth
   ¼ cup water
   4 teaspoons chicken stock base
     Pinch each of thyme and rosemary
     Garlic or onion salt and pepper to taste
   ¼ cup chopped parsley

Wash zucchini; trim off ends; slice thin. Wipe mushrooms with damp sponge or cloth; remove tough portion of stems; slice mushrooms thin. Combine zucchini and mushrooms in 10-inch Teflon skillet; add wine, water, and chicken stock base. Stir over medium heat until mixture becomes steamy; cover, turn heat low, and cook about 10 minutes, or just until vegetables are tender, shaking pan gently from time to time. Before serving, season to taste; sprinkle with parsley. Serve in sauce dishes so all the good juices can be enjoyed.

SAVORY POT ROAST

(serves 8 / 325 calories per serving)

   3 pounds beef sirloin tip (as lean as
     possible), rolled and tied
   1 cup diced carrots
   1 cup diced onion
     Several sprigs parsley, snipped with
     scissors
   1 clove garlic, chopped or pressed
   1 cup water
   1 (8 oz.) can tomato sauce
   ¾ cup California Red Table Wine
   1 teaspoon beef stock base
   1 bay leaf
   5 whole peppercorns
   3 whole allspice
     Dash of thyme
     Salt to taste

Place meat in Dutch oven or 3-quart casserole with a tight-fitting lid. Scatter carrots, onion, parsley, and garlic around meat. Combine water, tomato sauce, wine, and remaining ingredients in a saucepan; bring to boil; pour over meat. Cover and bake in 350° oven about 3 hours, or until meat is tender, turning and basting meat occasionally. Remove from oven; let meat cool to room temperature in the liquid.

Remove cooled meat from liquid and strain out vegetables; place meat and vegetables in tightly covered container. Refrigerate. Pour liquid into a measuring pitcher or bowl; refrigerate several hours or overnight, until fat on top solidifies. (To hasten the process, set in the freezer briefly.)

To make gravy: Remove layer of fat from chilled liquid; add water if needed to make 2 cups. In a saucepan mix ½ cup or so of the liquid with 2 tablespoons instant-blending flour; add remaining liquid; stir over medium heat until mixture boils. Add vegetables and 1 table-spoon California Brandy; taste and correct seasoning, if necessary.

To serve: Slice pot roast; remove all visible fat. Heat slices very gently in the gravy. Size of portion: 4 ounces cooked meat and ⅓ cup gravy.

CHEESECAKE TART

(serves 8 / 116 calories per serving)

   1 envelope unflavored gelatin
   ½ cup undiluted evaporated skim milk
   2 eggs, separated
   6 tablespoons sugar
   ⅛ teaspoon salt
   ½ teaspoon each: grated lemon peel and
     orange peel
   1½ teaspoons lemon juice
   ¾ teaspoon vanilla
   ¼ teaspoon almond extract
   1½ cups low-fat cottage cheese
   2 tablespoons packaged graham cracker
     crumbs
   ⅛ teaspoon mixed cinnamon and nutmeg

In top of small double boiler, sprinkle gelatin over milk. Add egg yolks; stir until thoroughly blended. Place over hot water; cook, stirring about 5 minutes, or until gelatin is completely dissolved and mixture thickens slightly. Remove from heat. Stir in 3 tablespoons sugar, salt, grated peels, lemon juice, vanilla, and almond extract. Whirl cottage cheese in blender until smooth; gradually add gelatin mixture, whirling until ingredients are completely blended. Chill, if necessary, until mixture mounds slightly when dropped from tip of a spoon. Beat egg whites until stiff but not dry; gradually add remaining 3 tablespoons sugar; beat until very stiff. Carefully fold in gelatin-cheese mixture, blending until no trace of egg white remains. Turn mixture into a 9-inch pie plate; smooth top. Mix graham cracker crumbs and spices; sprinkle evenly over top of tart. Chill until firm.

MENU

13

(1200 calories)

BREAKFAST
(200 calories)

Orange Juice
(½ cup / 55 calories)

Chicken-Mushroom Spread
*(2 tablespoons canned chicken spread mixed with
¼ cup chopped mushrooms / 62 calories)*

Toast
(1 slice with 1 teaspoon diet margarine / 82 calories)
Black Coffee or Tea

LUNCH
(300 calories)

Tuna-Cheese Dreams*
and
Pear-Pineapple Salad with Amber Dressing*
or
Fishwich au Gratin* or Fishwich Parmesan*
and
Mixed Green Slaw*

Black Coffee or Tea

DINNER
(550 calories)

Half Grapefruit
(55 calories)

Veal Capistrano* or Veal Helena*
Carrots with Grapes*

Celery
*(chilled, crisp hearts or briefly-cooked,
diced celery / all-you-want)*

Ice Milk
(½ cup / 142 calories)

Wine Choice: California Rosé

Extra Foods for Non-Slimmers:

Breakfast: Scrambled egg

**Lunch: Pimiento-stuffed olives; apple turnover (frozen
or from the bakery)**

**Dinner: Spoonful of Tangy Dressing (page 43) on the
grapefruit; quick-cooking brown rice with the
veal; chocolate sauce on the ice milk**

The 12-calorie figure includes 100 calories for the 4-ounce glass of dry Table Wine and 50 calories for the *all-you-want* vegetables as listed on page 14 and used in the menus and recipes. Recipes are included for all dishes marked with an asterisk.

TUNA-CHEESE DREAMS

(serves 4 / 193 calories per serving)

 1 (6½ oz.) can diet-pack tuna, drained and
    flaked
½ cup shredded process American cheese
    (2 ounces)
⅓ cup plain low-fat yoghurt
 2 tablespoons chopped green onions
    (include some green tops)
 2 teaspoons California Dry Vermouth
½ teaspoon each: Worcestershire sauce,
    prepared mustard, and prepared
    horseradish
    Seasoned salt and pepper to taste
 4 slices bread
 2 teaspoons diet margarine
    Paprika

Mix tuna, cheese, yoghurt, onions, Vermouth, and seasonings. Toast bread slices on one side; spread margarine (½ teaspoon per slice), then tuna mixture (about ⅓
cup per slice) on untoasted side. Place on baking sheet;
bake in 450° oven about 10 minutes, or until tuna mixture is bubbly and nicely browned. (Or, broil 4 to 6
minutes, watching carefully!) Before serving, cut each
sandwich in half; sprinkle with paprika.

PEAR-PINEAPPLE SALAD,
AMBER DRESSING

(110 calories per serving, including dressing)

For each serving, line a salad plate with crisp greens *(all
you want)*. On greens place 1 slice juice-pack canned
pineapple; top pineapple with ½ cup fresh or calorie-
reduced canned pear slices. Over each salad spoon 1
tablespoon Amber Salad Dressing (page 70).

FISHWICH AU GRATIN

(serves 4 / 275 calories per serving)

 1 pound fillets of sole
½ cup California White Table Wine
 2 tablespoons finely chopped green onion
    Dash of thyme
    Seasoned salt and pepper to taste
 3 (¾ oz.) slices process American cheese,
    cut in 4 strips each
 4 slices toast
    Paprika
 4 lemon wedges

Place sole in shallow baking dish; pour wine over fish;
let stand ½ hour or so. Remove fish from dish; pour off
wine. Pat fish dry with paper towels; replace in dish.
Bake in 250° oven about 20 minutes, or just until fish
is white. Scatter onion over fillets; sprinkle with thyme,
salt, and pepper; top with cheese strips. Broil just long
anough to melt the cheese. Watch carefully! To serve,
place a portion of sole on a slice of toast; sprinkle with
paprika. Accompany with lemon wedges.

For an individual Fishwich, use ¼ pound (4 ounces)
sole, 2 tablespoons wine, 3 strips cheese, and onion,
thyme, salt and pepper to taste.

FISHWICH PARMESAN

(serves 4 / 275 calories per serving)

 1 pound fillets of sole
½ cup California White Table Wine
½ cup plain low-fat yoghurt
⅓ cup grated Parmesan cheese
 2 teaspoons dry shredded green onions or
    chopped chives
¼ teaspoon Worcestershire sauce
    Dash of thyme; seasoned salt to taste
 2 tablespoons cornflake crumbs
 4 slices toast
    Paprika

Place sole in shallow baking dish; pour wine over fish;
let stand ½ hour or so. Remove fish from dish; pour off
wine. Pat fish dry with paper towels; replace in dish.
Mix yoghurt, cheese, onions, Worcestershire sauce,
thyme, and salt; spread over fish; sprinkle with cornflake crumbs. Bake in 450° oven about 10 minutes, or
just until fish flakes when tested with a fork. Don't overcook! To serve, place a portion of sole on each slice of
toast; dust with paprika.

For an individual Fishwich, use ¼ pound (4 ounces)
sole, 2 tablespoons wine, 2 tablespoons yoghurt, 4 teaspoons Parmesan cheese, ½ teaspoon shredded green
onions or chives, plus seasonings to taste and 1½ teaspoons cornflake crumbs.

MIXED GREEN SLAW

(27 calories per serving, including dressing)

Combine equal parts of finely shredded or chopped cabbage and lettuce; add a generous amount of chopped parsley. (*All-you-want* vegetables, so amounts are up to you.) Toss salad with Green Onion Dressing (page 25), allowing 1 tablespoon (3 teaspoons) dressing per portion. Chill for an hour or so to permit flavor of dressing to permeate the greens. Before serving, toss, taste, and add a little seasoned salt and/or coarse pepper, if needed. A sprinkling of celery seed is good here, too. Be sure to serve very cold.

VEAL CAPISTRANO

(serves 3 / 296 calories per serving)

  1 **pound veal round steak, cut ½ inch thick**
  2 **tablespoons grated Parmesan cheese**
  1 **tablespoon diet margarine**
  1 **tablespoon instant-blending flour**
  ¾ **cup canned condensed consommé**
  ½ **cup California White Table Wine**
  2 **green onions, thinly sliced**
  2 **tablespoons chopped parsley**
  1 **tablespoon drained capers**
  1 **clove garlic, chopped or pressed**
  ½ **teaspoon Worcestershire sauce**
    Dash each of thyme and marjoram
    Salt and pepper to taste
  ¼ **pound fresh mushrooms, wiped clean and sliced thin**
  1 **tablespoon California Medium Sherry**

Remove skin and bone from veal; with meat tenderizer, mallet, or edge of heavy plate, pound veal until ¼ inch thick. Sprinkle 1 tablespoon cheese over meat and pat into surface; cover with waxed paper; pound in cheese thoroughly. Turn meat over; repeat with remaining cheese. Cut meat in manageable pieces. Melt margarine in 10-inch Teflon skillet; arrange meat in pan in single layer. Sauté until browned on one side; turn and brown on the other side. Blend flour with consommé; add to veal; add wine, onions, parsley, capers, garlic, and seasonings. Cover; simmer gently about 45 minutes, or until veal is fork-tender, turning pieces frequently. Ten minutes or so before veal is done, add mushrooms. Just before serving, add Sherry; taste and correct seasoning, if necessary. If gravy seems too thick at any time, thin with a little water.

VEAL HELENA

(serves 3 / 295 calories per serving)

  1 **pound veal round steak, cut ½ inch thick**
  1½ **tablespoons diet margarine**
  ½ **cup finely chopped onion**
  ½ **medium-sized green pepper, chopped fine**
  1 **clove garlic, chopped or pressed**
  1 **(8 oz.) can tomato sauce**
  ½ **cup California White Table Wine**
    Pinch each of rosemary, basil, and marjoram
  ½ **teaspoon chicken stock base**
    Salt and pepper to taste
  2 **tablespoons California Dry Vermouth**

Remove skin and bone from veal; with meat tenderizer, mallet, or edge of heavy plate, pound veal until ¼ inch thick. Cut meat in manageable pieces. Melt margarine in 10-inch Teflon skillet; arrange meat in pan in single layer. Sauté until browned on one side; turn and brown the other side. Remove meat from pan. Put onion, green pepper, and garlic in pan; sauté gently, stirring frequently for 5 minutes. Return meat to pan. Add tomato sauce, wine, herbs, chicken stock base, salt, and pepper. Cover; simmer gently about 45 minutes, or until veal is fork-tender. Turn pieces frequently; add a little water if needed to thin gravy during cooking. Before serving, add Vermouth; taste and correct seasoning. Sliced fresh or canned mushrooms may be added toward end of cooking time without adding calories, since they're an *all-you-want* vegetable.

CARROTS WITH GRAPES

(60 calories per serving)

For each serving, allow ½ cup diced carrots and ¼ cup halved fresh or water-pack canned grapes, or well-rinsed syrup-pack canned grapes. Cook carrots in an inch or so of boiling salted water just until tender; drain off all but a tablespoon or so of the liquid. Add grapes, ½ teaspoon diet margarine per serving, and a generous sprinkling of chopped chives or parsley; heat gently just until piping hot. Season with salt and pepper to taste.

MENU
14
(1200 calories)

BREAKFAST
(200 calories)

Grapefruit Juice
*(½ cup fresh or canned unsweetened
grapefruit juice / 50 calories)*

Sardines on Toast
*(⅓ of a 3¾-oz. can sardines, well drained;
serve on 1 slice toast spread with ½ teaspoon
diet margarine; sprinkle with lemon juice /
151 calories)*

Black Coffee or Tea

LUNCH
(300 calories)

Borsch Salad Ring*
with Horseradish Cream Dressing*
or
Asparagus Aspic* with Pimiento Cream Dressing*
Grilled Ham-Cheese Toasties*

Black Coffee or Tea

DINNER
(550 calories)

Jellied Consommé*
Coq au Vin* or Chicken Oriental*

Peas with Celery
(the frozen combination; ½ cup / 58 calories)

Crookneck Squash
(or another all-you-want vegetable)

Claret-Spiced Mandarin Oranges*

Wine Choice: California Claret

Extra Foods for Non-Slimmers:

Breakfast: Broiled tomato

Lunch: Marinated garbanzos; ice cream bar or "bon bons" for dessert

Dinner: Noodles with chopped chives or parsley; canned pineapple chunks added to Claret-Spiced Mandarin Oranges; slice of angel food cake with the fruit

The 1200-calorie figure includes 100 calories for the 4-ounce glass of dry Table Wine and 50 calories for the *all-you-want* vegetables as listed on page 14 and used in the menus and recipes. Recipes are included for all dishes marked with an asterisk.

BORSCH SALAD RING

(serves 6 / 52 calories per serving)

1½ envelopes (1 envelope plus 1½
   teaspoons) unflavored gelatin
½ cup California Red Table Wine
2 tablespoons sugar
2 teaspoons beef stock base
1 (1 lb.) can julienne beets
2 tablespoons California red wine vinegar
1 teaspoon prepared horseradish
   Dash of powdered cloves
   Salt and pepper to taste
½ cup finely cut celery
1 tablespoon grated onion

In saucepan, sprinkle gelatin over wine; stir over low heat 3 or 4 minutes, until gelatin is completely dissolved. Add sugar and beef stock base; stir until dissolved; remove from heat. Drain beets, reserving liquid; measure liquid; add water as needed to make 1¼ cups. Combine this liquid with the gelatin mixture; add vinegar, horseradish, cloves, salt, and pepper; chill. When mixture is the consistency of unbeaten egg white, fold in drained beets, celery, and onion. Turn into a 1-quart ring mold that has been rinsed with cold water, or into 6 individual molds or custard cups; chill until firm. Unmold on crisp salad greens *(all-you-want)*. Serve with Horseradish Cream Dressing (following). Dressing portion for this salad: 3 tablespoons.

ASPARAGUS ASPIC

(serves 4 / 54 calories per serving)

1½ envelopes (1 envelope plus 1½
   teaspoons) unflavored gelatin
¼ cup California Dry Vermouth
1 (10½ oz.) can condensed chicken broth
3 tablespoons California white wine
   tarragon vinegar
   Dash of Tabasco
   Salt to taste
1 (15 oz.) can asparagus spears, drained
   and cut in ¾-inch lengths, or 1¼ cups
   cut-up cooked fresh asparagus tips
¼ cup finely cut celery
2 tablespoons chopped pimiento
1 tablespoon each: chopped green onion
   and parsley

In saucepan, sprinkle gelatin over wine; add ¼ cup of the chicken broth; stir over low heat until gelatin is dissolved. Remove from heat. Add remaining chicken broth, vinegar, Tabasco, and salt; chill. When mixture is consistency of unbeaten egg white, fold in remaining ingredients. Turn into a 3-cup mold that has been rinsed with cold water, or into 4 individual molds or custard cups; chill until firm. Unmold on crisp salad greens; serve with Pimiento Cream Dressing (following). Dressing portion for this salad: 3 tablespoons.

HORSERADISH CREAM DRESSING

(13 calories per tablespoon)

1 pint low-fat cottage cheese
2 tablespoons prepared horseradish (or
   more or less to taste, depending on how
   zesty you want it)
2 tablespoons California white wine vinegar
1 teaspoon salt
   Dash of cayenne
2 tablespoons chopped chives (if you like)

Combine all ingredients except chives in blender; whirl until smooth. Turn into jar or bowl; stir in chives. Cover; chill at least 1 hour before serving. Makes 2 cups. Fine with beet and tomato salads. Also delicious with beef, in place of the usual horseradish sauce made with whipped cream or sour cream. An excellent keeper.

PIMIENTO CREAM DRESSING

(12 calories per tablespoon)

1 cup low-fat cottage cheese
2 tablespoons cultured buttermilk
1½ teaspoons California Dry Vermouth
1½ teaspoons California white wine vinegar
2 tablespoons chopped pimiento
1 tablespoon chopped onion
   Bit of garlic, if you like
¾ teaspoon seasoned salt
¼ teaspoon Worcestershire sauce
   Dash of Tabasco sauce

Combine all ingredients in blender; whirl until smooth. Cover; chill at least an hour to blend flavors. Makes 1¼ cups. This dressing has a beautiful color and a flavor that enhances any vegetable salad.

GRILLED HAM-CHEESE TOASTIES
(215 calories per serving)

For each serving, allow 1 slice bread, 1 tablespoon deviled ham, and 1 (1 oz.) slice process Swiss or American cheese. Toast bread on one side; spread untoasted side with deviled ham; top with cheese slice. Broil, watching carefully, or bake in 450° oven, until cheese melts. Dust with paprika; cut in halves or quarters.

JELLIED CONSOMMÉ
(46 calories per serving)

For each serving, allow ½ (10½ oz.) can condensed consommé; chill several hours. At serving time, spoon into bouillon cups or other suitable dishes; top with 2 teaspoons California Dry Sherry and sprinkling of chopped watercress or parsley. Serve with lemon wedges *(all-you-want)*.

COQ AU VIN
(serves 4 / 363 calories per serving)

- 1 tablespoon diet margarine
- 1 (2½ to 3 lb.) chicken, quartered
- 2 tablespoons chopped onion
- 1 heaping cup sliced fresh mushrooms, or 1 (4 oz.) can sliced mushrooms, drained
- ¾ cup California Red Table Wine
- 1 bay leaf
- ¼ teaspoon each: thyme and pepper
  Salt to taste
- 1 tablespoon instant-blending flour
- 3 tablespoons water
  Chopped parsley (all-you-want)

Melt margarine in 12-inch Teflon skillet; place chicken in pan, skin side down; sauté slowly until golden brown. Turn chicken skin side up; continue sautéing until browned on the underside. Add onion, mushrooms, wine, bay leaf, thyme, pepper, and salt. Cover; cook slowly 30 to 45 minutes, or until chicken is tender, turning and basting pieces occasionally. Remove chicken from pan. Blend flour and water; stir into pan juices; simmer, stirring, until sauce thickens. Taste and correct seasoning. Return chicken to pan; heat gently but thoroughly. Before serving, sprinkle with chopped parsley.

CHICKEN ORIENTAL
(serves 4 / 363 calories per serving)

- 1 (2½ to 3 lb.) frying chicken, quartered
- ¾ cup California Rosé
- 3 tablespoons soy sauce
- 2 tablespoons water
- 1 clove garlic, chopped or pressed
- 1 teaspoon grated fresh ginger root, or ½ teaspoon powdered ginger
- ½ teaspoon oregano
- 1 tablespoon brown sugar

Tuck wing tip of chicken under shoulder joint; place chicken, skin side up, in single layer in shallow baking pan, preferably 1 to 1½ inches deep. Chicken should fill pan without crowding or leaving any pan area exposed (9 by 13 inches is a good size). Mix all remaining ingredients; spoon half of mixture over chicken; bake in 400° oven 30 minutes. Turn chicken skin side down; spoon on half of remaining wine mixture; bake an additional 20 minutes. Turn chicken skin side up; spoon on remaining wine mixture; bake another 10 minutes, or until chicken is tender.

To barbecue: Marinate chicken in wine-herb mixture before grilling; baste with mixture during cooking.

CLARET-SPICED MANDARIN ORANGES
(serves 4 / 83 calories per serving)

Drain 2 (10½ oz.) cans water-pack mandarin oranges; place in a bowl; set aside. In small saucepan combine ½ cup California Claret or other Red Table Wine, ¼ cup sugar, ¼ teaspoon each of grated lemon peel and orange peel, 4 whole cloves, and 1 (3 in.) stick of cinnamon; bring to boil; simmer 5 minutes. Pour hot mixture over oranges; cover; chill several hours or overnight. At serving time, remove spices; place oranges in dessert dishes; spoon some of the wine over each portion.

MENU
15
(1200 calories)

BREAKFAST
(200 calories)

Orange Juice
(½ cup / 55 calories)

Hot or Dry Cereal
(¾ cup cooked instant or quick-cooking hot cereal, or 1 cup rice, corn, or wheat flakes; ½ cup non-fat milk; non-caloric sweetener, if desired / 144 calories)

Black Coffee or Tea

LUNCH
(300 calories)

Salad Plate:
Jellied Bouillon Ring*
or Jellied Clam-Chicken Broth Ring*
with
Seafood and Sliced Tomatoes

Green Gables Dressing*

Crisp Celery Hearts, Cucumber Sticks, and/or Radishes
(all-you-want relishes)

Golden Toast Strips or Rye Wafers
(3 Strips, page 28, or 3 wafers / 63 calories)

Peaches
(¾ cup sliced fresh or calorie-reduced canned peaches / 50 calories)

Black Coffee or Tea

DINNER
(550 calories)

Tomato Juice or Vegetable Juice Cocktail
(¾ cup / 35 calories)

Braised Beef Burgundy*
or Grecian Beef Stew* or Beef Stew Mexicano*

Noodles with Parmesan Cheese
(½ cup cooked wide noodles, 1 teaspoon diet margarine, and 1 tablespoon Parmesan cheese / 142 calories)

Green Beans with Mushrooms
(cooked or canned green beans, plus briefly-simmered or canned mushrooms; season with onion salt and a sprinkling of lemon juice; all-you-want)

Ice Milk
(½ cup / 142 calories)

Wine Choice: California Pinot Noir

Extra Foods for Non-Slimmers:

Breakfast: Cinnamon toast

Lunch: Cottage cheese seasoned with chopped chives and seasoned salt; macaroons with the peaches

Dinner: Cheese crackers with the juice cocktail; butterscotch topping and sprinkling of toasted almonds on the ice milk

The 1200-calorie figure includes 100 calories for the 4-ounce glass of dry Table Wine and 50 calories for the *all-you-want* vegetables as listed on page 14 and used in the menus and recipes. Recipes are included for all dishes marked with an asterisk.

JELLIED BOUILLON RING

(serves 6 / 42 calories per serving)

2½ envelopes (2 envelopes plus 1½
   teaspoons) unflavored gelatin
½ cup California White Table Wine
2 (10½ oz.) cans condensed bouillon
   (beef broth)
½ cup water
2 tablespoons California Dry Sherry
1 tablespoon lemon juice
1 teaspoon Worcestershire sauce
   Dash of Tabasco sauce
   Salt to taste

In a saucepan mix gelatin and white wine; stir over low heat 3 to 4 minutes, until gelatin is completely dissolved. Combine gelatin with all remaining ingredients; stir well. Pour into a 1-quart ring mold that has been rinsed with cold water; chill until firm. Unmold on a platter; garnish with crisp salad greens *(all-you-want)*.

To complete Salad Plate: Fill center of ring with 3 (4½ oz.) cans small shrimp (about 3 cups), 2 (7½ oz.) cans crabmeat (about 2 cups), or 2 (6½ oz.) cans diet-pack tuna (about 2 cups), drained and flaked. Surround ring with 3 medium-sized tomatoes, quartered, and 12 canned (not marinated) or cooked frozen artichoke hearts, halved. Serve with Green Gables Dressing (following).

Size of portion: ⅙ Jellied Bouillon Ring; ½ cup shrimp, or ⅓ cup crabmeat or tuna; 2 tomato quarters; 4 artichoke halves; 6 tablespoons dressing. Total calories for the salad: 189.

JELLIED CLAM-CHICKEN BROTH RING

(serves 6 / 42 calories per serving)

2½ envelopes (2 envelopes plus 1½
   teaspoons) unflavored gelatin
½ cup California White Table Wine
2 (8 oz.) bottles clam juice
1 cup canned condensed chicken broth
2 tablespoons lemon juice
1 tablespoon California white wine vinegar
½ teaspoon grated onion
½ teaspoon Worcestershire sauce
   Dash of Tabasco sauce
   Salt to taste

In a saucepan mix gelatin and wine; stir over low heat 3 to 4 minutes, until gelatin is completely dissolved. Combine gelatin with all remaining ingredients; stir well. Pour into a 1-quart ring mold that has been rinsed with cold water; chill until firm. Unmold on a platter; garnish with crisp salad greens *(all-you-want)*.

To complete Salad Plate: Follow directions given in recipe for Jellied Bouillon Ring. Size of portion will be the same. Total calories for the salad: 189.

GREEN GABLES DRESSING

(8 calories per tablespoon)

1½ pints (3 cups) plain low-fat yoghurt
¼ cup California Dry Vermouth
2 tablespoons California white wine
   tarragon vinegar
2 tablespoons anchovy paste
2 teaspoons Dijon mustard
2 teaspoons lemon juice
½ teaspoon Worcestershire sauce
½ cup chopped parsley
2 tablespoons each: chopped chives and
   green onion (or ¼ cup of either)
2 cloves garlic, chopped or pressed
   Generous pinch of tarragon
   Salt and coarse black pepper to taste

Combine yoghurt, Vermouth, vinegar, anchovy paste, mustard, lemon juice, and Worcestershire sauce in a mixing bowl; beat with fork or wire whisk until thoroughly blended. Stir in remaining ingredients. Cover; chill an hour or more so flavors can blend. Makes 3½ cups. Excellent with seafood, vegetable, and green salads.

BRAISED BEEF BURGUNDY

(serves 6 / 230 calories per serving)

- 2 **pounds beef round or rump (as lean as possible), cut in 1-inch cubes**
- ½ **cup diced onion**
- ½ **cup diced carrots**
- 1 **clove garlic, chopped or pressed**
- 2 **tablespoons chopped parsley**
- 1 **(10½ oz.) can condensed bouillon (beef broth)**
- 1 **cup California Red Table Wine**
- ½ **bay leaf**
- 3 **whole allspice**
  Dash each of thyme and marjoram
  Salt and pepper to taste

Place meat in 2-quart casserole with tight-fitting lid; add onion, carrots, garlic, and parsley. Combine remaining ingredients in a saucepan; bring to a boil; pour over meat. Cover; bake in 350° oven about 3 hours, or until meat is tender. Remove from oven. Let meat cool to room temperature in the liquid.

Remove cooled meat and diced vegetables from liquid; place in tightly covered container; refrigerate. Pour liquid into a 1-pint measure; refrigerate several hours or overnight, until top layer of fat solidifies. (To hasten the process, set in the freezer.)

To make gravy: Remove layer of fat from chilled liquid; add water if needed to make 2 cups. Mix ½ cup or so of the liquid with 2 tablespoons instant-blending flour; combine with remaining liquid in a saucepan; stir over medium heat until mixture boils. Taste and correct seasoning, if necessary.

To serve: Add meat and diced vegetables to the gravy; heat thoroughly. Size of portion: 4 ounces meat and approximately ⅓ cup gravy.

GRECIAN BEEF STEW

(serves 6 / 231 calories per serving)

- 2 **pounds beef round or rump (as lean as possible), cut in 1-inch cubes**
- ½ **cup diced onion**
- ½ **cup diced carrots**
- 1 **clove garlic, chopped or pressed**
- ⅛ **unpeeled orange (wedge)**
- 1 **(2-in.) strip lemon peel**
- 1¼ **cups tomato juice**
- 1 **cup California Red Table Wine**
- 6 **whole cloves**
- 1 **stick cinnamon**
  Salt and pepper to taste

Place meat in 2-quart casserole with tight-fitting lid; add onion, carrots, garlic, orange, and lemon peel. Combine remaining ingredients in a saucepan; heat to boiling; pour over meat. Cover; bake in 350° oven about 3 hours, or until meat is tender. Remove from oven. Discard orange, lemon peel, cloves, and cinnamon stick. Let meat cool to room temperature in the liquid.

To finish dish: Refrigerate ingredients, make gravy, and serve as directed in the recipe for Braised Beef Burgundy (given). Size of portion: 4 ounces meat and approximately ⅓ cup gravy.

BEEF STEW MEXICANO

(serves 6 / 232 calories per serving)

- 2 **pounds beef round or rump (as lean as possible), cut in 1-inch cubes**
- 1 **cup diced onion**
- 1 **medium-sized green pepper, seeded and diced**
- 1 **clove garlic, chopped or pressed**
- 1 **(8 oz.) can tomato sauce**
- ¾ **cup California Red Table Wine**
- ½ **cup water**
- 1 **teaspoon beef stock base**
- 1 **teaspoon chili powder**
- ½ **teaspoon each: cumin seed and oregano**
  Salt to taste

Place meat in 2-quart casserole with tight-fitting lid; add onion, green pepper, and garlic. Combine remaining ingredients in a saucepan; bring to a boil; pour over meat. Cover and bake in a 350° oven about 3 hours, or until meat is tender. Remove from oven. Let meat cool to room temperature in the liquid.

To finish dish: Refrigerate ingredients, make gravy, and serve as directed in the recipe for Braised Beef Burgundy (given). Size of portion: 4 ounces meat and approximately ⅓ cup gravy.

MENU
16
(1200 calories)

BREAKFAST
(200 calories)

Half Grapefruit
(55 calories)

Monterey Jack Cheese
(1 ounce / 102 calories)

Rye Wafers
(2 wafers / 42 calories)
or
Toast
*(½ slice with ½ teaspoon diet margarine /
42 calories)*

Black Coffee or Tea

LUNCH
(300 calories)

**Chicken Livers with Artichoke Hearts
and Mushrooms* on Toast**

Lemony Beet Salad
*(page 50; serve ⅓ cup beet mixture per person
in lettuce cup / 34 calories)*

Black Coffee or Tea
or
Layered Mushroom-Pâté-Mold*
Beet and Artichoke Salad*

Rye Wafers or Saltines
*(4 wafers or 5-2" crackers with 1 teaspoon diet
margarine / 102 calories)*

Black Coffee or Tea

DINNER
(550 calories)

Tropical Cocktail Salad*

**Panned Fish Fillets with Green Herb Sauce*
and Crusty Baked Tomato***
or
Baked Fish Italiano*

Corn with Celery
*(for each serving, allow ⅓ cup kernels cut from
cooked corn or drained canned whole-kernel corn;
mix with briefly-cooked, diced celery,
all-you-want; season; heat gently / 48 calories)*

Angel Food Cake
(¹⁄₁₂ of 8" cake / 108 calories)

Wine Choice: California Chablis

Extra Foods for Non-Slimmers:

Breakfast: Crisp bacon

**Lunch: Lemon-flavored gelatin dessert made with apri-
cot nectar instead of water and topped with
frozen whipped dessert topping**

**Dinner: Canned shoestring potatoes with the fish;
scoop of vanilla ice milk on the cake, plus
fudge or pineapple ice cream topping**

The 1200-calorie figure includes 100 calories for the 4-ounce glass of dry Table Wine and 50 calories for the *all-you-want* vegetable as listed on page 14 and used in the menus and recipes. Recipes are included for all dishes marked with an asterisk.

CHICKEN LIVERS WITH ARTICHOKE HEARTS AND MUSHROOMS

(serves 4 / 262 calories per serving)

- ½ pound fresh mushrooms
- 1 tablespoon diet margarine
- 1 pound chicken livers, cut in bite-size pieces
- 2 tablespoons finely chopped onion
- 2 tablespoons instant-blending flour
- ¾ cup water
- ½ cup California Red Table Wine
- ½ teaspoon each: lemon juice and Worcestershire sauce
- ...ock base
- ...easoned salt and
- ...en artichoke hearts,
- ...ia Dry Sherry
- ...d parsley

...mp sponge or cloth; remove ...e mushrooms thin. Melt mar-...let; add chicken livers; sauté ...nutes, turning often. Remove ...ooms and onion in pan; stir ...til steamy, then cover and ...aking pan frequently. Blend ...shrooms; add red wine; cook, ...s and thickens. Add season-ings; just before ... return chicken livers to pan; add artichoke hearts, Sherry, and parsley; heat piping hot but do not boil. Serve on toast.

LAYERED MUSHROOM-PÂTÉ MOLD

(serves 6 / 124 calories per serving)

Mushroom Layer:
- 2 (4 oz.) cans sliced mushrooms
- ¼ cup California Dry Sherry
- 1 envelope unflavored gelatin
- ¾ cup canned condensed bouillon
- 2 teaspoons lemon juice
- ¾ teaspoon Worcestershire sauce
- 2 tablespoons chopped parsley

Drain mushrooms, reserving liquid. In small saucepan, combine ½ cup mushroom liquid and Sherry; sprinkle in gelatin; stir over low heat 3 or 4 minutes, until gelatin dissolves. Remove from heat. Stir in bouillon, lemon juice, and Worcestershire sauce. Mix mushrooms and parsley; spread evenly over bottom of a loaf pan (9 by 5 by 3½ inches). Spoon gelatin mixture over mushrooms; chill until firm.

Pâté Layer:
- 1 envelope unflavored gelatin
- ¼ cup cold water
- 1 pound chicken livers
- ½ cup California White Table Wine
- ½ cup canned condensed bouillon
- 2 tablespoons chopped onion
- 1 clove garlic
- 1 teaspoon Worcestershire sauce
- Dash each of thyme and nutmeg
- Salt and pepper to taste

Soften gelatin in the water. In saucepan, combine chicken livers, wine, bouillon, onion, and garlic; bring to boil; cover and simmer gently about 5 minutes, or just until livers are tender. Remove from heat. Add softened gelatin; stir until dissolved. Pour mixture into blender container; whirl until smooth. Add seasonings; whirl again. Cool mixture thoroughly at room temperature; spread evenly over firm mushroom layer. Chill until pâté is firm. To serve, unmold on a serving plate; decorate with sprigs of watercress or parsley (no added calories).

BEET AND ARTICHOKE SALAD

(74 calories per serving, including dressing)

To serve 6, allow 1 (1 lb.) can julienne beets and 1 (9 oz.) package frozen artichoke hearts. Drain beets; cook and drain artichokes; chill both vegetables. To serve, spoon beets onto lettuce-lined salad plates; top with artichoke hearts. Sprinkle with Tangy Dressing (page 43), allowing 2 tablespoons per portion.

TROPICAL COCKTAIL SALAD
(86 calories per serving)

For each serving, allow ⅓ of a papaya or ⅓ medium-sized cantaloupe, ⅓ cup diced fresh pineapple or ¼ cup drained juice-pack canned pineapple chunks, and 2 teaspoons Tangy Dressing (page 43). Marinate the pineapple in the dressing for 1 hour or so. At serving time, place papaya or cantaloupe on lettuce-lined salad plate; arrange marinated pineapple in hollow of the fruit; pour any dressing left from marinating over all.

PANNED FISH FILLETS WITH GREEN HERB SAUCE
(serves 3 / 266 calories per serving)

- 1 pound fillets of sole (thawed if frozen)
- 1 cup California White Table Wine
- 2 tablespoons instant-blending flour
- 2 tablespoons diet margarine
  Seasoned salt, pepper, and paprika
- ½ cup snipped parsley sprigs
- 4 green onions (white part only), thinly sliced
  Bit of garlic (if you like)
  Dash of thyme
  Lemon wedges *(all-you-want)*

Place fish in single layer in shallow baking dish; pour wine over it; let stand an hour or so. Just before cooking, remove fish from dish; measure and reserve ¾ cup liquid. Pat fish dry with paper towels. Spread flour in pie plate or other shallow dish; dip fish in flour, coating both sides. (Discard any leftover flour.) Melt margarine in Teflon skillet; put fish in pan in single layer; sprinkle with salt, pepper, and paprika. Sauté over low heat 2 or 3 minutes, just until pale golden on the underside. Turn fish carefully; sprinkle with salt, pepper, and paprika; sauté another 2 or 3 minutes, until pale golden on the other side. Add reserved wine marinade; cover; simmer very gently about 5 minutes, or just until fish flakes when tested with a fork, shaking pan gently several times.

While fish is cooking, chop parsley, onions, and garlic together until very, very fine. Remove cooked fish from skillet; place on heated dinner plates. Add chopped mixture and thyme to pan juices; stir well, heat to bubbling, and spoon over fish. Serve at once with lemon wedges and Crusty Baked Tomato (following).

CRUSTY BAKED TOMATO
(40 calories per serving)

For each serving, allow ½ medium tomato and 1 teaspoon each: diet margarine and packaged cornflake crumbs. Cut unpeeled tomato crosswise in halves; place, cut side up, in shallow Teflon baking pan. Season with seasoned salt, pepper, and dash of basil or oregano; dot with margarine; sprinkle with cornflake crumbs. Bake in 375° oven about 20 minutes.

BAKED FISH ITALIANO
(serves 4 / 307 calories per serving)

- 1½ pounds fillets of sole (thawed if frozen)
- 2 medium-sized fresh tomatoes, peeled, seeded, and cut in eighths, or use 2 thoroughly drained canned tomatoes
- 6 green onions (white part only) thinly sliced
- ½ cup snipped parsley sprigs
- 2 tablespoons chopped green pepper
- 1 clove garlic, sliced
- ¾ cup California White Table Wine
- 1 tablespoon instant-blending flour
  Generous pinch of oregano
  Salt and pepper to taste
- 1 tablespoon diet margarine
- 2 tablespoons (6 teaspoons) grated Parmesan cheese

Arrange fish in single layer in shallow baking dish; tuck tomato wedges around fish. Combine onions, parsley, green pepper, and garlic in chopping bowl; chop together until very, very fine. Stir wine and flour together until blended; add chopped mixture; season with oregano, salt and pepper; spoon mixture over fish and tomatoes. Dot with margarine. Bake in 375° oven 25 to 30 minutes, or until fish is tender, basting occasionally. Remove from oven; let rest 5 minutes or so before serving. Place fish and tomatoes on heated dinner plates; spoon sauce over; sprinkle each serving with 2 teaspoons Parmesan cheese.

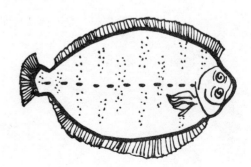

MENU

17

(1200 calories)

BREAKFAST
(200 calories)

Grapefruit Juice
*(½ cup fresh or canned unsweetened juice /
50 calories)*

Tuna on Toast
*(¹/₃ of a 6½-oz. can diet-pack tuna mixed
with 1 tablespoon plain low-fat yoghurt and
seasonings to taste; spread on 1 slice toast /
148 calories)*

Black Coffee or Tea

LUNCH
(300 calories)

Cottage Cheese Mousse*
with
Fruit or Vegetable Salad*

Rye Wafers or Golden Toast Strips
(3 wafers or 3 Strips, page 28 / 63 calories)
or
Ham Roll-Ups*
with
Fruit or Vegetable Salad*

Rye Wafers or Golden Toast Strips
(2 wafers or 2 Strips, page 28 / 42 calories)

Black Coffee or Tea

DINNER
(550 calories)

Consommé Madrilène*
Rabbit Sauté*
or
Rock Cornish Game Hens with Orange Sauce*

Swiss Chard
*(all-you-want; season with a sprinkling
of lemon juice)*

Crookneck or Pattypan Squash
(all-you-want)

Cocoa Banana
*(for each serving, slice 1 medium banana into
dessert dish; sprinkle with 1 teaspoon California
Sweet Sherry, ½ teaspoon each powdered
cocoa and sugar / 118 calories)*

Wine Choice: California Dry Sauterne

Extra Foods for Non-Slimmers:

Breakfast: Hard-cooked egg

Lunch: Avocado slices; raspberry sherbet for dessert

Dinner: Kasha (buckwheat groats) or bulgur (cracked
wheat) with the rabbit or Cornish hens; frozen
whipped dessert topping on Cocoa Banana

The 1200-calorie figure includes 100 calories for the 4-ounce glass of dry Table Wine and 50 calories for the *all-you-want* vegetables as listed on page 14 and used in the menus and recipes. Recipes are included for all dishes marked with an asterisk.

COTTAGE CHEESE MOUSSE

(serves 4 / 120 calories per serving)

1 envelope unflavored gelatin
¼ cup cold water
1 pint low-fat cottage cheese
½ cup cultured buttermilk
1 tablespoon California white wine vinegar
¼ teaspoon prepared horseradish (optional; omit if mousse is to be served with fruit)
⅛ teaspoon paprika
   Seasoned salt to taste
1 tablespoon chopped chives or parsley

In small saucepan, combine gelatin and water; stir over low heat 3 or 4 minutes, until gelatin is completely dissolved; set aside. In blender combine cottage cheese, buttermilk, vinegar, horseradish, and paprika; whirl until smooth. Add dissolved gelatin and salt; whirl until blended. Stir in chives or parsley. Pour into 4 individual molds or 6-ounce custard cups, or into a 3-cup mold; chill until firm.

At serving time, line a luncheon plate with crisp salad greens *(all-you-want)*; unmold Cottage Cheese Mousse on greens alongside a serving of Fruit Salad (following); spoon Amber Fruit Salad Dressing (following) over fruit. Or, accompany the Mousse with a serving of Vegetable Salad (following) and spoon Tangy Dressing (page 43) over vegetables.

Fruit Salad: (118 calories per serving, including dressing). For each serving, allow 1 slice juice-pack canned pineapple and ½ cup fresh or calorie-reduced canned pear slices. Place pineapple on greens; top with pear slices; add 4 teaspoons Amber Fruit Salad Dressing (following).

Vegetable Salad: (116 calories per serving, including dressing). For each serving, allow ½ medium tomato, 3 medium spears cooked broccoli, 2 well-drained anchovy fillets, and 2 large or 3 small ripe olives. Peel and slice tomato; arrange on greens and top with broccoli spears; crisscross anchovy fillets over broccoli; add 1½ tablespoons (4½ teaspoons) Tangy Dressing (page 43). Garnish plate with ripe olives.

HAM ROLL-UPS

(182 calories per serving)

For each serving, allow 2 (1 oz.) slices boiled ham and ¼ cup low-fat cottage cheese. Flavor cottage cheese with a sprinkling of chopped chives or green onion, and, if you like, a bit of prepared horseradish. (These flavorings won't add enough calories to count.) Spread 2 tablespoons cheese on each ham slice; roll up; chill, covered, an hour or more. At serving time, line a luncheon plate with crisp salad greens; place Roll-Ups on greens alongside a serving of Fruit Salad (following); spoon Amber Fruit Salad Dressing (following) over fruit. Or, accompany the Roll-Ups with a serving of Vegetable Salad (following) and spoon Tangy Dressing (page 43) over the vegetables.

Fruit Salad: (79 calories per serving, including dressing). For each serving, allow 1 slice juice-pack canned pineapple and 2 fresh or drained calorie-reduced canned apricot halves. Place pineapple on greens; top with apricots; add 3 teaspoons (1 tablespoon) Amber Fruit Salad Dressing (following). Crisp celery hearts can complete this plate at no extra calorie cost.

Vegetable Salad: (79 calories per serving, including dressing). For each serving, allow ½ medium tomato, 3 canned (not marinated) or cooked frozen artichoke hearts, and any amount of cooked or canned green beans that you like. Peel and slice tomato; arrange on greens with the artichoke hearts and beans. Add 2 tablespoons Tangy Dressing (page 43).

AMBER FRUIT SALAD DRESSING

(9 calories per teaspoon, 27 per tablespoon)

½ cup canned apricot nectar
¼ cup California Sweet Vermouth
1 tablespoon California white wine vinegar
2 tablespoons vegetable salad oil
1 teaspoon grated onion
½ teaspoon salt
¼ teaspoon each: paprika and dry mustard
2 teaspoons sugar

Combine all ingredients in a jar or bowl; shake or beat to mix well. Chill, covered, for at least an hour to blend flavors. Always shake or beat well before serving. Makes 1 cup. Delightful with any fruit salad.

CONSOMMÉ MADRILÈNE

(serves 4 / 38 calories per serving)

In saucepan mix 1 (10½ oz.) can condensed consommé, 1 cup tomato juice, 1 teaspoon lemon juice, dash of Tabasco sauce, and salt to taste. Bring to a boil; add 2 tablespoons California Dry Sherry. Pour into heated bouillon cups; float a paper-thin slice of lemon in each cup; sprinkle with chopped chives or parsley.

RABBIT SAUTÉ

(serves 4 / 398 calories per serving)

1 (2½ to 2¾ lb.) rabbit, cut up
1 tablespoon flour
1 tablespoon diet margarine
  Salt, pepper, and paprika to taste
  Generous dash each of thyme and
    marjoram
½ cup chopped onion
½ clove garlic, chopped or pressed
    (or use garlic salt)
½ cup California White Table Wine
3 tablespoons chopped parsley

Lay pieces of rabbit on a sheet of waxed paper; sprinkle with half the flour; turn pieces over and repeat with rest of flour. Roll pieces gently on the paper to take up any remaining flour. Melt margarine in a Teflon skillet; place rabbit in pan; sauté slowly until golden brown. Turn rabbit; continue sautéing until browned on the side. Sprinkle with salt, pepper, paprika, thyme, and marjoram; add onion and garlic; pour wine over all. Cover; cook slowly about 45 minutes, or until rabbit is tender, turning and basting pieces occasionally. Before serving, sprinkle with chopped parsley.

ROCK CORNISH GAME HENS WITH ORANGE SAUCE

(serves 4 / 397 calories per serving)

2 (approx. 1 lb. 6 oz.) Rock Cornish game
    hens
  Salt and pepper
2 thick slices onion
2 stalks celery, halved crosswise
6 tablespoons California Sweet Vermouth
2 tablespoons diet margarine
½ cup hot water
1 teaspoon chicken stock base
1 tablespoon cornstarch
1 tablespoon plus 1 teaspoon sugar
½ cup orange juice
1 tablespoon California red wine vinegar
1 teaspoon grated orange peel
1 (10½ oz.) can water-pack mandarin
    oranges, drained

Sprinkle cavities of hens with salt and pepper; put a slice of onion and 2 pieces of celery in each bird; spoon 1 tablespoon of the Vermouth into each one. Place hens in a heavy casserole or Dutch oven with tight-fitting lid; hens should fit rather snugly, without too much space left over. Spread 1 tablespoon diet margarine on each bird; sprinkle with salt and pepper. Cover; bake in 450° oven 1 hour, or until birds are tender.

Remove hens from casserole; set aside. Pour off and discard any drippings from casserole. Put hot water in casserole; add chicken stock base; stir until dissolved. Continue stirring and scraping bottom and sides of casserole to catch any little brown bits left from roasting; pour this liquid into a saucepan. Mix cornstarch and sugar; gradually add orange juice, blending until smooth; add mixture to broth in saucepan. Stir over medium heat until mixture boils, thickens, and becomes clear. Remove from heat. Add remaining 4 tablespoons Vermouth, vinegar, and orange peel; season to taste with salt and pepper; stir in oranges. Replace hens in casserole; spoon sauce over them. Bake, uncovered, in 350° oven 15 minutes, basting several times with the sauce.

To serve, cut hens in half with poultry shears or sharp kitchen shears; place, cut side down, on heated dinner plates; spoon sauce over them. Garnish with sprigs of watercress or parsley *(all-you-want)*.

BREAKFAST
(200 calories)
Vegetable Juice Cocktail
(¾ cup / 35 calories)

Frankfurter
(1 all-meat frankfurter, 10-to-a-lb. / 133 calories)

Toast
(½ slice toast spread with prepared mustard / 33 calories)

Black Coffee or Tea

LUNCH
(300 calories)

Baked Stuffed Mushrooms with Crabmeat*
or
Baked Stuffed Mushrooms with Tuna*

Spinach-Cheese Tart*

Crisp Radishes
(all-you-want)

Rye Wafers or Toast Strips
(2 wafers or 2 Strips, page 28 / 42 calories)

Black Coffee or Tea

DINNER
(550 calories)

Tossed Grape and Mushroom Salad*

Remi's Veal Sauté* or Veal Madras*

Zucchini
*(all-you-want season with onion and/or garlic salt;
add plenty of chopped parsley)*

Rice
*(½ cup cooked long-grain white rice, mixed or
sprinkled with 2 teaspoons grated Parmesan cheese;
add some briefly cooked all-you-want celery,
if desired / 107 calories)*

Mandarin Marmalade Compote*

Wine Choice: California Grey Riesling

Extra Foods for Non-Slimmers:

Breakfast: Bacon wrapped around frankfurter and grilled

Lunch: Sliced tomatoes with Tangy Dressing (page 43); pear for dessert

Dinner: Chutney, chopped peanuts, raisins, and any other favorite curry condiments with Veal Madras; sour half and half on Mandarin Marmalade Compote

The 1200-calorie figure includes 100 calories for the 4-ounce glass of dry Table Wine and 50 calories for the *all-you-want* vegetables as listed on page 14 and used in the menus and recipes. Recipes are included for all dishes marked with an asterisk.

BAKED STUFFED MUSHROOMS WITH CRABMEAT

(serves 3 / 115 calories per serving)

12 fresh mushrooms, approx. 2 inches in
   diameter
2 tablespoons finely cut green onion
   (include some green tops)
3 tablespoons California Dry Vermouth
1 (7½ oz.) can crabmeat, drained and
   flaked (approx. 1 cup)
¼ cup plain low-fat yoghurt
3 tablespoons grated Parmesan cheese
½ teaspoon Worcestershire sauce
   Seasoned salt and pepper to taste
   Paprika

Wipe mushrooms with damp cloth or sponge. Remove stems; chop stems fine. Combine stems, onion, and Vermouth in saucepan; cover; simmer 5 minutes, stirring 2 or 3 times. Uncover; simmer until any liquid is evaporated; remove from heat. Combine this mixture with the crabmeat, yoghurt, 2 tablespoons Parmesan cheese, Worcestershire sauce, salt, and pepper; mound filling in mushroom caps. Place in shallow baking pan greased with tiny dab (⅛ teaspoon) diet margarine; sprinkle with remaining 1 tablespoon Parmesan cheese and paprika. Cover, using foil if pan has no lid; bake in 350° oven 15 minutes. Uncover; bake 5 minutes longer.

BAKED STUFFED MUSHROOMS WITH TUNA

(serves 3 / 115 calories per serving)

Follow recipe for Baked Stuffed Mushrooms with Crabmeat, substituting 1 (6½ oz.) can diet-pack tuna for the crabmeat.

SPINACH-CHEESE TART

(serves 3 / 143 calories per serving)

1 (10 oz.) package frozen chopped spinach
1 cup low-fat cottage cheese
3 tablespoons grated Parmesan cheese
1 egg, slightly beaten
2 green onions, finely cut (include some
   green tops)
   Generous pinch of basil
   Salt and pepper to taste

Cook spinach according to package directions; turn into strainer; press with rubber spatula or back of spoon to drain thoroughly. Mix spinach, cottage cheese, and Parmesan cheese; add remaining ingredients. Spread mixture in 8-inch pie plate greased with a tiny dab (⅛ teaspoon) diet margarine; bake in 350° oven 30 minutes. Remove from oven; let stand 10 to 15 minutes before serving.

TOSSED GRAPE AND MUSHROOM SALAD

(69 calories per serving)

For each serving, allow ¼ cup halved fresh or water-pack canned seedless grapes, ⅓ cup thinly sliced raw mushrooms, 4 teaspoons White Wine Dressing (page 79), and any amount of shredded, crisp salad greens you like. Combine grapes, mushrooms, and dressing in a bowl; cover; chill an hour or so. At serving time, combine grape mixture with greens, tossing lightly. Taste and add a little salt if needed. Serve on chilled salad plates.

If fresh and water-pack canned grapes are both unobtainable, you can substitute canned syrup-pack grapes. Rinse them quickly under running water; halve and use as directed.

REMI'S VEAL SAUTÉ

(serves 4 / 282 calories per serving)

½ pound fresh mushrooms
1 tablespoon diet margarine
1½ pounds veal shoulder, cut in 1-inch
    cubes
½ medium-sized green pepper, slivered
2 green onions thinly sliced (include
    some green tops)
1 clove garlic, chopped or pressed
2 medium-sized tomatoes, peeled and cut
    in eighths
½ cup California White Table Wine
    Pinch of rosemary
    Seasoned salt and pepper to taste
1 tablespoon instant-blending flour
¼ cup California Dry Vermouth
1 (9 oz.) package frozen artichoke
    hearts, cooked and drained, or
    8 canned (not marinated) artichoke
    hearts, rinsed, drained, and halved
2 tablespoons chopped parsley

Wipe mushrooms with damp sponge or cloth; remove tough portion of stems; slice mushrooms thin; set aside. Melt margarine in 10-inch Teflon skillet; add meat and sauté over medium heat until browned, turning to brown all sides. Remove meat from skillet. Put mushrooms, green pepper, onions, and garlic in pan; sauté gently 5 minutes, stirring frequently. Return meat to pan; add tomatoes, white wine, rosemary, salt, and pepper. Cover; simmer gently about 1½ hours, or until meat is tender, stirring often. Blend flour and Vermouth; stir into contents of skillet; heat, stirring, until sauce thickens. Add artichoke hearts and parsley; taste and correct seasoning before serving.

MANDARIN ORANGE COMPOTE

(serves 4 / 90 calories per serving)

3 tablespoons orange marmalade
¼ cup orange juice
2 tablespoons California Brandy
2 (10½ oz.) cans water-pack mandarin
    oranges

Combine marmalade, orange juice, and Brandy, blending well. Drain oranges; place in a bowl; pour marmalade mixture over them. Cover; chill several hours or overnight, stirring occasionally. To serve, place oranges in dessert dishes; spoon some of the sauce over each portion.

VEAL MADRAS

(serves 4 / 284 calories per serving)

1 tablespoon diet margarine
1½ pounds veal shoulder, cut in
    1-inch cubes
½ cup each: diced carrot, onion,
    and celery
1 clove garlic, chopped or pressed
1½ cups boiling water
½ cup California White Table Wine
1 teaspoon chicken stock base
1 bay leaf
4 whole peppercorns
    Pinch of thyme
    Salt to taste
2 tablespoons instant-blending flour
1 teaspoon curry powder (or to taste)
2 tablespoons California Medium Sherry

Melt margarine in 10-inch Teflon skillet; add meat and sauté over medium heat until browned, turning to brown all sides. Add carrot, onion, celery, garlic, boiling water, white wine, chicken stock base, bay leaf, peppercorns, thyme, and salt. Cover; simmer gently about 1½ hours, or until meat is tender, stirring often.

Remove meat and vegetables from broth. Measure broth; add water as needed to make 1¼ cups; pour back into skillet. Blend flour and curry powder with ¼ cup cold water; add to broth in skillet; cook, stirring, until mixture boils and thickens. Return meat and vegetables to skillet; add Sherry; taste and correct seasoning, if necessary. Heat gently before serving.

BREAKFAST
(200 calories)

Tomato Juice
(¾ cup / 35 calories)

Poached Egg on English Muffin
(toast ½ English muffin; spread with ½ teaspoon diet margarine; top with 1 poached egg / 162 calories)

Black Coffee or Tea

LUNCH
(300 calories)

Papaya or Cantaloupe Salad with Shrimp*
or
Fruited Chicken Salad*

Golden Toast Strips or Rye Wafers
(4 Strips, page 28, or 4 wafers / 84 calories)

Black Coffee or Tea

DINNER
(550 calories)

Eggplant-Zucchini Appetizer*
Herb-Crusted Roast Lamb*
or
Wine-Basted Roast Lamb* with Mint Sauce*

Spinach
(¾ cup cooked spinach, seasoned with lemon pepper / 30 calories)

Rice with Mushrooms
(½ cup cooked long-grain white rice, mixed with all the drained canned or briefly simmered sliced mushrooms you wish, plus ½ teaspoon diet margarine / 100 calories)

Apricot Cloud*

Wine Choice: California Zinfandel

Extra Foods for Non-Slimmers:

Breakfast: Canadian bacon

Lunch: French or crescent rolls; ice cream bar or "bon bons" for dessert

Dinner: Crackers or rye wafers with Eggplant-Zucchini Appetizer; mint jelly with the lamb

The 1200-calorie figure includes 100 calories for the 4-ounce glass of dry Table Wine and 50 calories for the *all-you-want* vegetables as listed on page 14 and used in the menus and recipes. Recipes are included for all dishes marked with an asterisk.

PAPAYA OR CANTALOUPE SALAD WITH SHRIMP

(215 calories per serving, including dressing)

For each serving, allow ½ papaya or ½ small cantaloupe, ¾ cup cooked or canned small shrimp, and ⅓ cup Seafood Sauce Louise (page 28). Line a luncheon or salad plate with crisp greens *(all-you-want)*. Peel and slice the papaya or cantaloupe; arrange slices on greens. Top fruit with shrimp; spoon dressing over all. Be sure all ingredients are very cold. Crisp, tender celery hearts can go along on the plate with no added calories.

FRUITED CHICKEN SALAD

(serves 6 / 215 calories per serving)

2 cups diced, cooked white meat of chicken
1 cup diced heart of celery
¾ cup halved fresh or drained water-pack canned seedless grapes (or well-rinsed syrup-pack grapes)
¼ cup thinly sliced pimiento-stuffed olives
1 cup Creamy Cottage Cheese Dressing (following)
   Seasoned salt to taste
   Crisp salad greens
12 slices juice-pack canned pineapple
   Chopped parsley or paprika

Combine chicken, celery, grapes, and olives in a bowl; toss lightly to mix. Add dressing; stir gently to coat all ingredients. Cover; chill at least 1 hour, preferably 2 or 3. Before serving, stir gently again; taste and add seasoned salt, if needed. To serve, line each luncheon or salad plate with crisp greens *(all you want)*; place 2 pineapple slices on the greens; top pineapple with a serving (½ cup) of chicken salad; sprinkle with parsley or paprika.

A good way to prepare the chicken for this salad (or any dish calling for cooked chicken) is to buy chicken breasts and poach them in the oven. For 2 cups diced meat you will need approximately 1½ pounds chicken breasts. Arrange them, skin side up, in a shallow pan; sprinkle with seasoned salt and pepper; pour in just enough water to cover bottom of pan; cover loosely with aluminum foil. Bake in 325° oven 1 hour, basting occasionally. Let cool; remove bones and skin; dice meat with scissors.

CREAMY COTTAGE CHEESE DRESSING

(12 calories per tablespoon, 192 per cup)

1¼ cups low-fat cottage cheese
¼ cup cultured buttermilk
1½ teaspoons California Dry Vermouth
1½ teaspoons California white wine tarragon vinegar
2 green onions, sliced (include some green tops)
2 tablespoons snipped parsley sprigs
1 small clove garlic, halved
1 teaspoon seasoned salt
¼ teaspoon each: Worcestershire sauce and dill weed
   Coarse pepper to taste

Combine all ingredients in blender; whirl until smooth. Cover; chill at least 1 hour to blend flavors. Makes 1½ cups. Very good with vegetable and seafood salads, as well as chicken.

EGGPLANT-ZUCCHINI APPETIZER

(serves 6 / 23 calories per serving)

1 medium-sized eggplant (about 1¼ lbs.)
1 (8 oz.) can zucchini in tomato sauce
3 tablespoons finely chopped parsley
1 tablespoon California red wine vinegar
¼ teaspoon mixed Italian seasoning
   Garlic salt, onion salt, and coarse black pepper to taste

Cook whole, unpeeled eggplant, covered, in boiling water about 20 minutes, or until soft; drain. When cool enough to handle, peel and combine in chopping bowl with the zucchini; chop until vegetables are very fine. Add remaining ingredients; mix well. Cover; chill thoroughly before serving in crisp lettuce cups. Makes about 2 cups.

HERB-CRUSTED ROAST LAMB

(serves 8 or more / 270 calories per serving)

    1 leg of lamb, boned and rolled (approx.
        4 lbs. ready-to-cook weight)
    ¼ cup Dijon prepared mustard
    1 tablespoon soy sauce
    1 tablespoon California Dry Vermouth
    1 clove garlic, chopped
    1 teaspoon rosemary

An hour or so before roasting time, place lamb on a rack in a shallow baking pan. In a small bowl mix mustard, soy sauce, Vermouth, garlic, and rosemary; using a pastry brush, paint lamb on all sides with the mixture. Insert meat thermometer in center. Roast in 325° oven, allowing 25 to 30 minutes per pound if you like your lamb pink (150-155° on meat thermometer), 35 to 40 minutes per pound (175-180°) if you like it well done. Remove roast to a carving board or platter and let rest while you make Pan Sauce (following). Size of portion: 4 ounces lamb (lean only) and 3 tablespoons sauce. Total: 279 calories.

Pan Sauce for Lamb: Pour off all drippings from roasting pan. Into the pan pour ¾ cup each California Red Table Wine and canned condensed consommé; heat to boiling, stirring to loosen any little crusty bits from the pan. Pour sauce into a small saucepan; keep warm over low heat. Add any meat juices that escape during carving; season with salt and pepper; serve piping hot with the lamb. Makes 1½ cups, plus meat juices; count as 3 calories per tablespoon.

WINE-BASTED ROAST LAMB

(serves 6 to 8 / 270 calories per serving)

    1 (4 to 5 lb.) leg of lamb
    2 tablespoons California Medium Sherry
    1 clove garlic, chopped or pressed
    1 teaspoon each: rosemary and paprika
    ½ teaspoon basil
    1 cup California White Table Wine
    ½ cup canned chicken broth (not
        condensed)

An hour or so before roasting time, place lamb fat side up on a rack in a shallow baking pan. In a small bowl mix Sherry, garlic, rosemary, paprika, and basil; using

a pastry brush, paint lamb all over with the mixture. Insert meat thermometer in thickest part of roast, away from bone. Roast in 325° oven, allowing 20 to 25 minutes per pound (150-155° on meat thermometer) if you like your lamb pink, 30 to 35 minutes per pound (175°-180°) if you like it well done. Mix white wine and chicken broth; use to baste lamb every 20 minutes or so, until mixture is gone. The meat's own juices make a delicious sauce for this roast, or for a few extra calories you can enjoy a spoonful of Mint Sauce (following). Size of portion: 4 ounces meat (lean only) and 2 tablespoons Mint Sauce. Total: 280 calories.

Mint Sauce: In small saucepan, mix ⅔ cup water, ½ cup California white wine vinegar, 2 tablespoons sugar, and dash of salt; bring to boil, stirring until sugar is dissolved. Remove from heat; stir in ⅓ cup finely chopped fresh mint. Cover; let stand several hours so flavor can mellow. Serve at room temperature. Makes about 1⅓ cups; 5 calories per tablespoon. This sauce keeps indefinitely; store, covered, in the refrigerator.

APRICOT CLOUD

(serves 6 / 99 calories per serving)

    1 envelope unflavored gelatin
    1 (12 oz.) can apricot nectar
    ⅓ cup sugar
        Dash of salt
    2 tablespoons lemon juice
    2 egg whites
    6 teaspoons (2 tablespoons) California
        Muscatel

In a small saucepan, sprinkle gelatin over ½ cup apricot nectar; stir over low heat about 3 minutes, until gelatin is dissolved. Add sugar and salt; stir until dissolved. Remove from heat. Add remaining apricot nectar and lemon juice; chill until mixture begins to thicken. Beat egg whites stiff; fold in partially thickened gelatin mixture, blending gently until no trace of egg white remains. Pour into serving bowl; chill until firm, stirring gently several times at first to prevent separation. When serving, spoon 1 teaspoon Muscatel over each portion. Top each portion with 1 tablespoon frozen whipped dessert topping (16 calories).

MENU
20
(1200 calories)

BREAKFAST
(200 calories)

Vegetable Juice Cocktail
(¾ cup / 35 calories)

Chipped Beef on Toast
(spread 1 slice toast with ½ teaspoon diet margarine, then with prepared mustard; top with 1½ ounces chipped beef / 161 calories)

Black Coffee or Tea

LUNCH
(300 calories)

Pineapple-Cucumber Salad Molds*
or
Sherried Grapefruit Salad Molds*
White Wine Salad Dressing*
Harlequin Cottage Cheese*

Golden Toast Strips or Rye Wafers
(2 Strips, page 28, or 2 wafers / 42 calories)

Black Coffee or Tea

DINNER
(550 calories)

Shrimp and Celery Cocktail*
with Seafood Sauce Louise

Baked Deviled Chicken*
or
Baked or Barbecued Chicken El Dorado*
Artichoke Hearts and Mushrooms Sauté*
Cherried Peaches*

Wine Choice: California Pinot Blanc

Extra Foods For Non-Slimmers:

Breakfast: Monterey Jack or Swiss cheese

Lunch: Avocado slices with the salad; brownie or date bar for dessert

Dinner: Baked banana with the chicken; slice of angel food cake with the fruit

The 1200-calorie figure includes 100 calories for the 4-ounce glass of dry Table Wine and 50 calories for the *all-you-want* vegetables as listed on page 14 and used in the menus and recipes. Recipes are included for all dishes marked with an asterisk.

PINEAPPLE-CUCUMBER SALAD MOLDS

*(serves 4 / 156 calories per serving,
including dressing)*

1 (15¼ oz.) can juice-pack crushed
   pineapple
1 envelope unflavored gelatin
½ cup California White Table Wine
2 tablespoons sugar
¼ teaspoon salt
2 tablespoons California white wine vinegar
1 tablespoon lemon juice
½ medium cucumber, peeled, seeded, and
   finely diced
2 tablespoons chopped pimiento
1 teaspoon grated onion

Drain and reserve juice from pineapple. (Empty contents of can into a strainer; set over a bowl; press with back of spoon to extract juice.) In saucepan combine gelatin and wine; stir over low heat 3 or 4 minutes, until gelatin is completely dissolved. Add sugar and salt; stir until dissolved. Add pineapple juice, vinegar, and lemon juice; chill. When mixture begins to thicken, stir in drained pineapple, cucumber, pimiento, and onion. Pour into 4 individual molds or 6-ounce custard cups that have been rinsed with cold water; chill until firm. Unmold on crisp salad greens; serve with White Wine Dressing (following). Dressing portion for this salad: 4 teaspoons.

SHERRIED GRAPEFRUIT SALAD MOLDS

*(serves 4 / 157 calories per serving,
including dressing)*

1 (1 lb.) can juice-pack grapefruit sections
½ cup canned apricot nectar
¼ cup California Sweet Vermouth
1 envelope unflavored gelatin
2 tablespoons sugar
¼ teaspoon salt
2 teaspoons lemon juice
¼ cup finely cut celery
¼ cup thinly sliced pimiento-stuffed olives
1 teaspoon grated onion

Drain grapefruit sections, reserving juice; cut sections in half. Combine nectar and wine in a saucepan; sprinkle in gelatin; stir over low heat 3 or 4 minutes, until gelatin dissolves. Add sugar and salt; stir until dissolved. Add grapefruit juice and lemon juice; chill. When mixture begins to thicken, fold in grapefruit sections, celery, olives, and onion. Spoon into 4 individual molds or 6-ounce custard cups that have been rinsed with cold water; chill until firm. Unmold on crisp salad greens; serve with White Wine Dressing (following). Dressing portion for this salad: 4 teaspoons.

WHITE WINE SALAD DRESSING

(10 calories per teaspoon, 30 per tablespoon)

½ cup California White Table Wine
1 tablespoon California white wine vinegar
2 tablespoons salad oil
1 tablespoon lemon juice
2 tablespoons chopped parsley
½ clove garlic, chopped or pressed
¾ teaspoon salt
½ teaspoon Worcestershire sauce
¼ teaspoon each: dry mustard, paprika,
   and coarse pepper

Combine all ingredients in a jar or bowl; shake or beat to mix well. Chill, covered, for at least an hour to blend flavors. Always shake or beat well before serving. Makes ¾ cup. Excellent with mixed green, vegetable, and many fruit salads.

HARLEQUIN COTTAGE CHEESE

(serves 4 / 104 calories per serving)

To serve 4, allow 1 pint low-fat cottage cheese, 2 tablespoons grated green pepper, 2 tablespoons grated raw carrot, 2 finely chopped green onions (include some green tops), and seasoned salt and pepper to taste. Mix all ingredients; chill before serving. Size of portion: ½ cup.

SHRIMP AND CELERY COCKTAIL

(serves 4 / 68 calories per serving)

Mix 1 (4½ oz.) can (1 cup) small shrimp and ½ cup finely cut celery; divide among 4 lettuce-lined cocktail cups. Spoon 3 tablespoons Seafood Sauce Louise (page 28) over each portion; sprinkle with parsley or paprika. Serve with lemon wedges. The secret of good flavor here is to have shrimp, celery, and sauce all well chilled.

BAKED DEVILED CHICKEN

(serves 4 / 380 calories per serving)

1 (2½ to 3 lb.) frying chicken, quartered
½ cup catsup
½ cup California White Table Wine
1 tablespoon California white wine vinegar
1 tablespoon Worcestershire sauce
1 tablespoon grated onion
1 teaspoon seasoned salt
¼ teaspoon dried fines herbes
2 tablespoons chopped chives or parsley

Tuck wing tip of chicken under shoulder joint; place chicken, skin side up, in single layer in shallow baking pan, preferably 1 to 1½ inches deep. Chicken should fill pan without crowding or leaving any pan area exposed (9 by 13 inches is a good size). Mix all remaining ingredients except chives or parsley; spoon half of mixture over chicken, bake in 400° oven 30 minutes. Turn chicken skin side down; spoon on half of remaining catsup-wine mixture; bake an additional 20 minutes. Turn chicken skin side up; spoon on remaining catsup-wine mixture; bake another 10 minutes, or until chicken is tender. Before serving, sprinkle with chives or parsley.

BAKED OR BARBECUED CHICKEN EL DORADO

(serves 4 / 375 calories per serving)

1 (2½ to 3 lb.) frying chicken, quartered
1 teaspoon chicken stock base
¼ cup hot water
½ cup California White Table Wine
¼ cup lemon juice
1 tablespoon vegetable salad oil
1 teaspoon Worcestershire sauce
2 tablespoons each: finely chopped green onions and parsley
1 clove garlic, chopped or pressed
½ teaspoon each: paprika, rosemary, and oregano

Arrange chicken in pan as directed in recipe for Baked Deviled Chicken (given). Dissolve chicken stock base in hot water; add all remaining ingredients. Spoon half of wine mixture over chicken; bake in 400° oven 30 minutes. Turn chicken skin side down; spoon on half of remaining wine mixture; bake additional 20 minutes. Turn chicken skin side up; spoon on remaining wine mixture; bake another 10 minutes, or until chicken is tender.

To barbecue: Marinate chicken in wine-herb mixture an hour or more before grilling; baste with the mixture during cooking.

ARTICHOKE HEARTS AND MUSHROOMS SAUTÉ

(serves 4 / 20 calories per serving)

½ pound fresh mushrooms
1 tablespoon finely chopped onion
2 tablespoons California Dry Vermouth
1 teaspoon lemon juice
½ teaspoon chicken stock base
1 (9 oz.) package frozen artichoke hearts, cooked and drained
Seasoned salt and/or garlic salt and pepper to taste
2 tablespoons finely chopped parsley

Wipe mushrooms with damp sponge or cloth; cut off tough portion of stems; slice mushrooms thin. Put mushrooms and onion in Teflon skillet; sprinkle with Vermouth, lemon juice, and chicken stock base; stir over medium-high heat until mixture is steamy. Cover; turn heat low; continue cooking 5 minutes, shaking pan occasionally. Add artichoke hearts, salt, and pepper; mix lightly. Before serving, sprinkle with chopped parsley.

CHERRIED PEACHES

(84 calories per serving)

For each serving, allow ½ cup pitted dark, sweet cherries (fresh, unsweetened frozen, or canned calorie-reduced), ½ peach (fresh or canned calorie-reduced), and 1 tablespoon California Port. Mix cherries and Port; cover; chill at least 1 hour. At serving time, peel fresh peach or drain canned peach; place, cut side up, in dessert dish. Put cherries in hollow of peach; spoon wine over all.

MENU

21

(1200 calories)

BREAKFAST
(200 calories)

Strawberries
(1 cup capped fresh or unsweetened frozen berries / 53 calories)

Hot or Dry Cereal
(¾ cup instant or quick-cooking hot cereal, or 1 cup rice, corn, or wheat flakes; ½ cup non-fat milk; non-caloric sweetener, if desired / 144 calories)

Black Coffee or Tea

LUNCH
(300 calories)

Shrimp-Artichoke Luncheon Casserole*
or Crab-Artichoke Luncheon Casserole*
or Tuna-Artichoke Luncheon Casserole*

Crisp Radishes
(all-you-want)

Toast
(1 slice with ½ teaspoon diet margarine / 74 calories)

Black Coffee or Tea

DINNER
(550 calories)

**Tossed Green Salad with Bean Sprouts
and Mushrooms***
with
Red Wine Dressing*

Beef and Vegetable Torta*
or Beef and Spinach Loaf with Tomato Sauce*

Polenta
(²/₃ cup cooked cornmeal mixed or sprinkled with 2 teaspoons grated Parmesan cheese / 98 calories)

Ambrosia*

Wine Choice: California Claret

Extra Foods for Non-Slimmers:

Breakfast: Toast with jam or marmalade

Lunch: Relish tray of cherry tomatoes and ripe olives; lime sherbet for dessert

Dinner: Frozen petite peas or baby lima beans; gingersnaps with Ambrosia

The 1200-calorie figure includes 100 calories for the 4-ounce glass of dry Table Wine and 50 calories for the *all-you-want* vegetables as listed on page 14 and used in the menus and recipes. Recipes are included for all dishes marked with an asterisk.

SHRIMP-ARTICHOKE LUNCHEON CASSEROLE

(serves 3 / 227 calories per serving)

½ cup evaporated skim milk, or ⅓ cup
    powdered skim milk and ½ cup water
½ cup canned condensed chicken broth
2 tablespoons instant-blending flour
1 tablespoon diet margarine
1 ounce (¼ cup) shredded Cheddar cheese
¼ teaspoon each: Worcestershire sauce
    and grated lemon peel
    Seasoned salt and pepper to taste
2 tablespoons California Dry Sherry
1 (9 oz.) package frozen artichoke hearts,
    cooked and drained
1½ cups cooked small shrimp, or 1½
    (4½ oz.) cans, drained
1 cup finely diced celery or thinly sliced
    fresh mushrooms, simmered 5 minutes
    in a little water and drained, or 1 (4
    oz.) can sliced mushrooms, drained
2 tablespoons grated Parmesan cheese
    Paprika

In a saucepan combine milk (or powdered milk and water), chicken broth, and flour; stir over medium heat until mixture boils and thickens. Add margarine and Cheddar cheese; stir over low heat until melted and blended with the sauce. Add seasonings and Sherry. Arrange artichoke hearts in a single layer in a shallow casserole (or 3 individual casseroles); scatter shrimp and celery (or mushrooms) over artichokes; spoon sauce over all; sprinkle with Parmesan cheese and paprika. Bake in 400° oven about 15 minutes, or until piping hot.

CRAB-ARTICHOKE LUNCHEON CASSEROLE

(serves 3 / 227 calories per serving)

Follow recipe for Shrimp-Artichoke Luncheon Casserole; substitute 1 cup fresh crabmeat or 1 (7½ oz.) can crabmeat, drained, for the shrimp.

TUNA-ARTICHOKE LUNCHEON CASSEROLE

(serves 3 / 227 calories per serving)

Follow recipe for Shrimp-Artichoke Luncheon Casserole; substitute 1 (6½ oz.) can diet-pack tuna, drained and flaked, for the shrimp.

TOSSED GREEN SALAD WITH BEAN SPROUTS AND MUSHROOMS

(40 calories per serving, including dressing)

For each serving, allow all you like of chilled salad greens, fresh or drained canned bean sprouts, and thinly sliced raw, cooked, or canned mushrooms; add 1 thinly sliced green onion. Toss together in a salad bowl; add Red Wine Dressing (following); toss again. Dressing portion for this salad is 4 teaspoons.

RED WINE SALAD DRESSING

(10 calories per teaspoon, 30 per tablespoon)

½ cup California Red Table Wine
2 tablespoons California red wine tarragon
    vinegar
2 tablespoons vegetable salad oil
½ clove garlic, chopped or pressed
¾ teaspoon salt
½ teaspoon Worcestershire sauce
¼ teaspoon each: dry mustard, paprika,
    and coarse pepper

Combine all ingredients in a jar or bowl; shake or beat to mix well. Chill, covered, for at least an hour to blend flavors. Always shake or beat well before serving. Makes ¾ cup. Excellent with mixed green, vegetable, and many fruit salads.

BEEF AND VEGETABLE TORTA

(serves 6 / 273 calories per serving)

1 pound small zucchini
½ cup chopped onion
¼ cup California Dry Vermouth
1 pound lean ground beef
1 (10 oz.) package frozen chopped spinach,
    cooked and thoroughly drained
2 eggs, well beaten
¼ cup evaporated skim milk
½ cup fine, dry bread crumbs
⅔ cup grated Parmesan cheese
1 clove garlic, chopped or pressed
¼ teaspoon each: rosemary and oregano
    Pinch of allspice
    Seasoned salt and pepper to taste

Wash zucchini and trim off ends; cook whole in boiling salted water about 10 minutes, or just until tender. Drain; chop coarsely; drain again. Combine onion and Vermouth in a Teflon skillet; stir over medium heat until mixture is steamy, then cover, turn heat low, and cook 5 minutes, or until onion is tender and wine has evaporated. Remove onion from pan. In the same pan, sauté beef until it is no longer red, stirring with a fork to separate it into bits. Drain meat thoroughly. Combine meat, onion, and zucchini; add all remaining ingredients except 2 tablespoons of the cheese. Spoon mixture into a 9-inch pie plate; smooth top; sprinkle with reserved cheese. Bake in 350° oven 45 minutes, or until knife inserted near center comes out clean. Remove from oven; let stand 10 minutes or so before cutting. Serves 6.

BEEF AND SPINACH LOAF

(serves 6 / 275 calories per serving)

1 egg, slightly beaten
½ cup evaporated skim milk
½ cup water
3 slices white bread, crumbled
1¼ pounds lean ground beef
1 (10 oz.) package frozen chopped spinach,
    cooked and thoroughly drained
½ cup finely chopped onion
    Bit of chopped or pressed garlic
2 tablespoons grated Parmesan cheese
1½ teaspoons seasoned salt
½ teaspoon mixed Italian seasoning
½ teaspoon pepper
1 (8 oz.) can tomato sauce
3 tablespoons California Dry Vermouth

In a large mixing bowl combine egg, milk, water, and bread crumbs; let stand 5 minutes or so; blend well with a fork. Add meat, spinach, onion, garlic, cheese, and seasonings; mix well. Pack into a loaf pan (8½ x 4½ x 2½ inches); bake in 350° oven 45 minutes. Remove from oven; carefully pour off liquid from pan. Mix tomato sauce and wine; spoon ½ cup of mixture over loaf. Return to oven; bake 25 minutes longer. Remove from oven; let stand 2 or 3 minutes; again pour off all liquid from pan. Heat remaining tomato sauce-wine mixture to simmering; serve as a sauce with the meat loaf. Size of portion: ⅙ of the loaf, 1½ tablespoons tomato sauce.

AMBROSIA

(127 calories per serving)

For each serving allow ½ cup fresh orange segments, ¼ teaspoon grated orange peel, 1 tablespoon California Muscatel, ⅓ cup ripe banana slices, and 1 teaspoon shredded coconut. Combine orange segments, orange peel, and wine; cover; chill. Just before serving, add banana slices; mix lightly; top with coconut. Garnish, if desired, with a no-calorie sprig of fresh mint.

MENU

22

(1200 calories)

BREAKFAST
(200 calories)

Orange Nog
*(1 egg and ¾ cup orange juice whirled in
blender till foamy; add non-caloric sweetener,
if desired / 162 calories)*

Toast
(½ slice with ¼ teaspoon diet margarine / 37 calories)

Black Coffee or Tea

LUNCH
(300 calories)

Chicken Florentine*
or Chicken and Mushrooms Florentine*

Tomato Salad
(½ medium tomato on all-you-want *salad greens,
with 2 teaspoons Tangy Dressing, page 43 /
30 calories)*

Black Coffee or Tea
or
Chicken Canton* with Bean Sprouts

Golden Toast Strips or Rye Wafers
(3 Strips, page 28, or 3 wafers / 63 calories)

Mandarin Pineapple Salad*
Black Coffee or Tea

DINNER
(550 calories)

Clam Juice Cocktail*
Alsatian Frankfurters and Sauerkraut*
or
Oven-Barbecued Frankfurters* and Panned Cabbage*

Green Beans
(all-you-want)

Boiled Potato
*(1 medium, 3-to-a-lb., peeled before boiling, served
with ½ teaspoon diet margarine / 87 calories)*

Apple Fluff*

Wine Choice: California Gamay

Extra Foods for Non-Slimmers:

Breakfast: Deviled ham to spread on the toast

**Lunch: Crisp Chinese noodles; apricots (fresh or
canned) for dessert**

**Dinner: Gingerbread (made from a mix) with Apple
Fluff**

The 1200-calorie figure includes 100 calories for the 4-ounce glass of dry Table Wine and 50 calories for the *all-you-want* vegetables as listed on page 14 and used in the menus and recipes. Recipes are included for all dishes marked with an asterisk.

CHICKEN FLORENTINE

(serves 2 / 270 calories per serving)

½ cup undiluted evaporated skim milk
½ cup water
 2 tablespoons instant-blending flour
 1 teaspoon chicken stock base
 1 teaspoon diet margarine
⅛ teaspoon Worcestershire sauce
　Dash of nutmeg
　Seasoned salt and pepper to taste
 1 tablespoon California Dry Sherry
½ teaspoon each: chopped chives and
　parsley
 1 cup diced, cooked chicken
 1 (10 oz.) package frozen chopped spinach,
　cooked and thoroughly drained
 2 teaspoons grated Parmesan cheese
　Paprika

In saucepan combine milk, water, flour, chicken stock base, and margarine; stir over medium heat until mixture boils and thickens. Add seasonings, Sherry, chives, and parsley; stir chicken into sauce. Spread spinach in shallow casserole (or 2 individual casseroles); spoon chicken mixture over spinach; sprinkle with Parmesan cheese and paprika. Bake in 375° oven 15 minutes, or until piping hot.

CHICKEN AND MUSHROOMS FLORENTINE

(serves 2 / 270 calories per serving)

Simmer 1 heaping cup thinly sliced fresh mushrooms 5 minutes in covered pan with ¼ cup water; drain; add mushrooms to sauce along with chicken. Or, drain and add 1 (4 oz.) can sliced mushrooms. In either case, mushroom liquid can replace some or all of the water in the sauce. No added calories, since mushrooms are an *all-you-want* vegetable.

CHICKEN CANTON

(serves 3 / 184 calories per serving)

 2 tablespoons diet margarine
½ cup finely diced celery
¼ cup finely chopped onion
 2 tablespoons chopped green pepper
 2 tablespoons instant-blending flour
¾ cup canned condensed chicken broth
¼ cup California White Table Wine
 2 teaspoons soy sauce
　Salt and pepper to taste
 1 cup diced, cooked chicken
 1 (4 oz.) can mushrooms, drained, or
　1 heaping cup fresh mushrooms, sliced,
　simmered 5 minutes in ¼ cup water,
　and drained
¼ cup thinly sliced canned water chestnuts
　Fresh or canned bean sprouts

Melt margarine in saucepan; add celery, onion, and green pepper; sauté gently, stirring frequently, for 5 minutes. Blend flour with chicken broth; add to celery mixture; cook, stirring, until mixture boils and thickens. Add wine, soy sauce, salt, and pepper; stir in chicken, mushrooms, and water chestnuts; heat gently but thoroughly. Serve over hot bean sprouts (an *all-you-want* vegetable).

MANDARIN PINEAPPLE SALAD

(56 calories per serving, including dressing)

For each serving, allow 1 slice juice-pack canned pineapple and ¼ cup drained water-pack canned mandarin orange segments. Place pineapple on salad plate lined with sprigs of watercress or frilly lettuce leaves *(all-you-want)*; top with orange segments; spoon 1 teaspoon Amber Dressing (page 70) over the fruit. Serve very cold.

CLAM JUICE COCKTAIL

(serves 4 / 31 calories per serving)

To serve 4, mix 1 (8 oz.) bottle clam juice, 1 cup vegetable juice cocktail, 2 tablespoons catsup, 1 tablespoon lemon juice, 1 teaspoon Worcestershire sauce, and (if you like) a dash of Tabasco sauce. Cover; chill thoroughly. Stir well before serving.

ALSATIAN FRANKFURTERS AND SAUERKRAUT

(serves 4 / 336 calories per serving)

1 (1 lb. 11 oz.) can sauerkraut
1 cup chopped onion
1 clove garlic, chopped or pressed
½ bay leaf
1 tablespoon brown sugar
1 teaspoon beef stock base
1 teaspoon celery seed
2 cups canned chicken broth (not
    condensed)
½ cup California White Table Wine
    Salt and pepper to taste
8 all-meat frankfurters (10-to-a-lb. size)
    Chopped parsley

Drain sauerkraut; rinse well; drain again. Combine sauerkraut in a 10-inch skillet with onion, garlic, bay leaf, brown sugar, beef stock base, and celery seed; mix well. Pour in chicken broth and wine; season with salt and pepper. Bring to a boil; turn heat low and simmer gently, covered, for 2 hours, stirring occasionally. Lay frankfurters on top of sauerkraut mixture; continue cooking, covered, 10 minutes. To serve, mound sauerkraut (approx. 1 cup) on dinner plates; top each serving with 2 frankfurters; sprinkle with chopped parsley (*all-you-want*). Pass prepared mustard with this flavorsome dish. (One-half teaspoon mustard: approx. 4 calories.)

OVEN-BARBECUED FRANKFURTERS

(serves 4 / 322 calories per serving)

½ cup chopped onion
½ clove garlic, chopped or pressed
½ cup California White Table Wine
½ cup catsup
¾ cup water
2 tablespoons California white wine vinegar
2 teaspoons Worcestershire sauce
1 tablespoon sugar
½ teaspoon each: paprika, dry mustard,
    celery salt, and pepper
8 all-meat frankfurters (10-to-a-lb. size)

Combine onion, garlic, and wine in saucepan; cover; simmer gently 5 minutes. Add all remaining ingredients except frankfurters; mix well; heat to boiling. Split frankfurters lengthwise with sharp knife, cutting almost but not quite through them. Place frankfurters, split side up, in shallow pan; pour hot sauce over them. Bake in 350° oven 30 minutes, basting several times. Serve 2 frankfurters per person on a mound of Panned Cabbage (following), with some of the sauce spooned over each portion. Sprigs of parsley or watercress make a good no-calorie-count garnish for the plate.

Panned Cabbage: Melt 1 tablespoon diet margarine in 10-inch skillet; add 6 cups shredded cabbage, 1 cup very thinly sliced celery, 2 tablespoons finely chopped green pepper, 2 tablespoons water, a good sprinkling of celery seed, and seasoned salt and pepper to taste; stir well. Cover; steam over low heat about 7 minutes, just until cabbage is crisp-tender, stirring occasionally. Serve at once. Serves 4 / 13 calories per serving, since the vegetables are on the *all-you-want* list.

APPLE FLUFF

(serves 6 / 80 calories per serving)

¼ cup California Port
¾ cup cold water
1 envelope unflavored gelatin
¼ cup sugar
    Dash of salt
¼ teaspoon cinnamon
    Dash of nutmeg
1 teaspoon grated lemon peel
1 tablespoon lemon juice
2 cups unsweetened applesauce

In saucepan, combine Port and ¼ cup water; sprinkle in gelatin; stir over low heat 2 to 3 minutes, until gelatin dissolves. Remove from heat; stir in remaining ½ cup water, sugar, salt, spices, lemon peel, lemon juice, and applesauce. Chill, stirring occasionally, until mixture mounds slightly when dropped from tip of spoon; beat with rotary or electric beater until light and fluffy. Turn into 6 dessert dishes; chill until firm. At serving time, top each portion with 1 tablespoon frozen whipped dessert topping (16 calories).

BREAKFAST
(200 calories)

Vegetable Juice Cocktail
(¾ cup / 35 calories)

Poached Egg
(1 large egg / 80 calories)
on
Deviled Ham Toast
*(1 slice toast spread with
1½ teaspoons deviled ham / 88 calories)*

Black Coffee or Tea

LUNCH
(300 calories)

Shrimp Creole*

Green Beans or Zucchini
(all-you-want)

Rice
(½ cup cooked long-grain white rice / 91 calories)

Chilled Pineapple Chunks
*(½ cup juice-pack canned chunks with liquid /
64 calories)*

Black Coffee or Tea
or
Green Bean or Zucchini Salad
with
Tuna or Crabmeat Sauce*

Toast
(1 slice with 1 teaspoon diet margarine / 82 calories)

Chilled Pineapple Chunks
*(½ cup juice-pack canned chunks with liquid /
64 calories)*

Black Coffee or Tea

DINNER
(550 calories)

Asparagus Tips Vinaigrette*

Broiled or Barbecued Beefburgers*
with
Red Wine Sauce,* Red Wine-Mushroom Sauce,*
or Green Pepper and Onion Sauté*

Cauliflower Piquant*

Cinnamon Baked Bananas*

Wine Choice: California Zinfandel

Extra Foods for Non-Slimmers:

Breakfast: Toasted English muffin instead of toast, with
Hollandaise sauce (canned) over the egg

Lunch: Cup cake with the pineapple

Dinner: Scalloped or au gratin potatoes (frozen or packaged); vanilla ice milk or sour half and half on
the banana

The 1200-calorie figure includes 100 calories for the 4-ounce glass of dry Table Wine and 50 calories for the *all-you-want* vegetables as listed on page 14 and used in the menus and recipes. Recipes are included for all dishes marked with an asterisk.

SHRIMP CREOLE

(serves 4 / 148 calories per serving)

½ cup diced onion
½ cup diced celery
¼ cup chopped green pepper
1 clove garlic, chopped and pressed
1 teaspoon chicken stock base
½ cup California White Table Wine
1 (1 lb.) can stewed tomatoes
1 tablespoon instant-blending flour
2 bay leaves, crushed
¼ teaspoon each: thyme and basil
    Seasoned salt and pepper to taste
    Dash of cayenne
2½ cups cooked small shrimp, or 2½
      (4½ oz.) cans small shrimp, drained
2 tablespoons chopped parsley

Combine onion, celery, green pepper, garlic, chicken stock base, and wine in a saucepan or skillet. Stir over medium heat until mixture is steamy; cover, turn heat low, and simmer 5 minutes, stirring occasionally. Drain and reserve liquid from tomatoes; blend liquid and flour; stir into vegetable mixture. Add tomatoes and seasonings. Cover; simmer gently 15 minutes, stirring occasionally. Add shrimp; simmer, covered, 5 minutes longer. Before serving, taste and adjust seasoning; add parsley.

GREEN BEAN OR ZUCCHINI SALAD WITH TUNA OR CRABMEAT SAUCE

(151 calories per serving, including sauce)

For each serving, arrange a bed of crisp salad greens on a plate; on greens place ½ peeled medium-sized tomato; top tomato with a generous bundle of chilled, cooked or canned green beans or chilled, cooked zucchini strips. (Salad greens, green beans, and zucchini are *all-you-want* vegetables.) Just before serving spoon Tuna or Crabmeat Sauce (following) over the salad; dust with paprika. Sauce portion: ⅔ cup.

TUNA OR CRABMEAT SAUCE

(203 calories per cup)

1 cup plain low-fat yoghurt
1 tablespoon California Dry Vermouth
1 tablespoon catsup
½ teaspoon Worcestershire sauce
¼ teaspoon prepared horseradish
1 (6½ oz.) can diet-pack tuna or 1 (7½ oz.)
    can crabmeat, drained and flaked
2 tablespoons chopped pimiento
1 tablespoon well-drained sweet pickle
    relish
2 teaspoons each: chopped chives and
    parsley
¾ teaspoon seasoned salt
    Pepper to taste

Combine yoghurt, wine, catsup, Worcestershire sauce, and horseradish in a bowl; beat with fork or wire whisk until well blended. Stir in remaining ingredients. Cover; chill an hour or more to blend flavors. Makes 2 cups.

ASPARAGUS TIPS VINAIGRETTE

(65 calories per serving, including dressing)

For each serving, arrange 6 cooked or canned asparagus tips on crisp lettuce. Spoon 4 teaspoons Vinaigrette Dressing (following) over each portion:

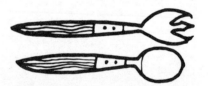

VINAIGRETTE DRESSING

(10 calories per teaspoon, 30 per tablespoon)

½ cup California White Table Wine
2 tablespoons California white wine
    tarragon vinegar
2 tablespoons vegetable salad oil
3 tablespoons chopped parsley
2 teaspoons chopped chives or green onions
2 teaspoons chopped, drained capers
1 teaspoon grated onion
½ clove garlic, chopped or pressed
¾ teaspoon salt
½ teaspoon Worcestershire sauce
¼ teaspoon each: dry mustard and coarse
    pepper

Combine all ingredients in a jar or bowl; shake or beat until well blended. Cover; chill at least an hour to blend flavors. Shake or stir well before serving. Makes a generous ¾ cup. A fine sauce for chilled vegetables. Also good as a dressing for seafood salads.

BROILED OR BARBECUED BEEFBURGERS

(serves 2 / 340 calories per serving)

¾ **pound (12 ounces) lean ground beef**
¾ **teaspoon seasoned salt**
¼ **teaspoon coarse black pepper**
¼ **cup California Red Table Wine**

Combine ingredients lightly with a fork. Shape into 2 equal-sized patties, or 4 smaller ones. Broil, panbroil in an ungreased Teflon skillet, or grill on the barbecue until done as you like them. Serve immediately with Red Wine Sauce, Red Wine-Mushroom Sauce, or Green Pepper and Onion Sauté (following).

RED WINE SAUCE

(serves 2 / 34 calories per serving)

½ **cup water**
⅓ **cup California Red Table Wine**
1 **tablespoon instant-blending flour**
¾ **teaspoon beef stock base**
1½ **teaspoons diet margarine**
1 **tablespoon chopped parsley**
2 **teaspoons chopped chives or**
   green onions
   Bit of chopped or pressed garlic
1 **teaspoon soy sauce**
½ **teaspoon Worcestershire sauce**
   Dash of thyme
   Seasoned salt and pepper to taste

In a small saucepan combine water, wine, flour, beef stock base, and margarine; stir over medium heat until mixture comes to a boil; turn heat low and simmer very gently for 4 to 5 minutes, stirring frequently. Add remaining ingredients; serve piping hot. Makes about ⅔ cup. Size of portion: ⅓ cup.

RED WINE-MUSHROOM SAUCE

(serves 2 / 34 calories per serving)

Follow recipe for Red Wine Sauce, using liquid from 1 (4 oz.) can sliced mushrooms in place of part of the required water. (Or, simmer 1 heaping cup thinly sliced fresh mushrooms, covered, in ¼ cup water 5 minutes; use liquid in place of part of the water.) Add mushrooms and ½ teaspoon lemon juice to sauce before serving. Makes about 1 cup. Size of portion: ½ cup. No added calories to count, since mushrooms are an *all-you-want* vegetable.

GREEN PEPPER AND ONION SAUTÉ

(serves 2 / 33 calories per serving)

1 **medium-sized green pepper**
1 **teaspoon diet margarine**
1 **cup thinly sliced onion**
1 **teaspoon beef stock base**
¼ **cup California Dry Vermouth**
¼ **cup water**
   Salt and pepper to taste
1 **tablespoon chopped parsley**

Cut a thin slice from stem end of green pepper; remove seeds and fibrous white portion; wash under running water. With a sharp knife, cut pepper in thin, short strips. Melt margarine in a Teflon skillet; add onion and green pepper; sprinkle with beef stock base; add wine and water. Stir over medium heat until mixture becomes steamy; cover, turn heat low, and simmer gently for 15 minutes, or until vegetables are very tender, stirring occasionally. Season to taste; add parsley just before serving. Makes about 1 cup. Size of portion: ½ cup. If you're a garlic fancier, you can add a bit here at no extra calorie cost.

CAULIFLOWER PIQUANT

(an all-you-want vegetable)

Trim and wash a head of cauliflower; separate into flowerets. Cook in 1-inch boiling salted water to which you have added 1 teaspoon mixed pickling spice, 1 tablespoon California white wine tarragon vinegar, 1 thick slice onion, and 1 peeled clove garlic. Cook to your taste... just don't overcook! This is an excellent treatment for vegetables that are to be served either hot or in salad. Try it with green beans, carrots, and pattypan squash, too.

CINNAMON BAKED BANANAS

(112 calories per serving)

For each serving, allow 1 medium-sized banana, 1 teaspoon each California Sweet Vermouth and orange juice, ½ teaspoon brown sugar, and a generous dusting of cinnamon. Peel banana and place in shallow baking dish; sprinkle with other ingredients. Bake in 375° oven 15 to 20 minutes or until tender. Serve warm.

BREAKFAST
(200 calories)

Tomato Juice or Vegetable Juice Cocktail
(¾ cup / 35 calories)

Ham on Toast with Prepared Mustard
*(1½ ounces thin-sliced boiled ham on
1 slice toast / 164 calories)*

Black Coffee or Tea

LUNCH
(300 calories)

Jellied Tuna Loaf* or Salmon Mousse*
with
Caper Cheese Dressing*

Green Bean and Tomato Salad*

Golden Toast Strips or Rye Wafers
(2 Strips, page 28, or 2 wafers / 42 calories)

Black Coffee or Tea

DINNER
(550 calories)

Half Grapefruit
(55 calories)

Baked Whole Chicken Rosemary*

Celery Hearts Romano*

Casserole Mushrooms*

Custard Mont Blanc*

Wine Choice: California Chablis

Extra Foods for Non-Slimmers:

Breakfast: Slice of cheese with the ham on toast

Lunch: Marinated artichoke hearts added to Green Bean and Tomato Salad; apple or pear for dessert

Dinner: Instant mashed potatoes with the chicken; cranberry sauce; spoonful of frozen whipped dessert topping on the custard

The 1200-calorie figure includes 100 calories for the 4-ounce glass of dry Table Wine and 50 calories for the *all-you-want* vegetables as listed on page 14 and used in the menus and recipes. Recipes are included for all dishes marked with an asterisk.

JELLIED TUNA LOAF

(serves 6 / 132 calories per serving)

    2 envelopes unflavored gelatin
    ½ cup California White Table Wine
    1 (10½ oz.) can condensed chicken broth
    ¾ cup water
    1½ tablespoons lemon juice
    1½ teaspoons Worcestershire sauce
       Salt and pepper to taste
    2 (6½ oz.) cans diet-pack tuna, drained
       and flaked
    2 hard-cooked eggs, grated or finely
       chopped
    ⅔ cup finely cut celery
    ¼ cup chopped parsley
    2 tablespoons chopped pimiento
    1 tablespoon grated onion

Sprinkle gelatin over wine in a saucepan; stir over low heat 3 or 4 minutes, until gelatin is dissolved. Add chicken broth, water, lemon juice, Worcestershire sauce, salt, and pepper. Chill. When mixture begins to thicken, fold in all remaining ingredients. Pour into a loaf pan (8½ by 4½ by 2½ inches) that has been rinsed with cold water. Chill until firm. Unmold on a platter and garnish with bunches of watercress or parsley *(all-you-want)*. Slice with a very sharp knife and serve with Caper-Cheese Dressing (following). Size of portion: ⅙ of loaf and 4 tablespoons dressing.

SALMON MOUSSE

(serves 6 / 146 calories per serving)   4. Carb.

    1½ envelopes (1 envelope plus 1½
       teaspoons) unflavored gelatin
    ½ cup California White Table Wine
    1 (1 lb.) can pink salmon
    1½ cups plain low-fat yoghurt
    1 tablespoon anchovy paste
    1 tablespoon California white wine
       tarragon vinegar
    1 tablespoon grated onion
    1 teaspoon lemon juice
    ½ teaspoon Worcestershire sauce
       Salt and pepper to taste
    1 cup finely diced celery
    ¼ cup chopped parsley

Sprinkle gelatin over wine in a saucepan; stir over low heat 3 or 4 minutes, until gelatin is dissolved. Drain salmon; remove bones and skin; flake very fine with a fork. Blend yoghurt and anchovy paste; add salmon. Gradually stir in gelatin mixture; add vinegar, onion, lemon juice, Worcestershire sauce, salt, and pepper. Chill. When mixture begins to thicken, fold in celery and parsley. Spoon mixture into a 1-quart ring mold or 6 individual molds or 6-ounce custard cups that have been rinsed with cold water. Chill until firm. Unmold on crisp salad greens *(all-you-want)*. Serve with Caper-Cheese Dressing (following). Size of portion: ⅙ of ring mold (or 1 individual mold or custard cup) and 3 tablespoons dressing.

CAPER-CHEESE DRESSING

(12 calories per tablespoon)   2.4 Carb.

    2 cups (1 pint) low-fat cottage cheese
    2 tablespoons cultured buttermilk
    1 tablespoon California Dry Vermouth
    1 tablespoon California white wine vinegar
    2 green onions, sliced (include some green
       tops)
    2 tablespoons snipped parsley sprigs
    1 tablespoon drained capers
    1 small clove garlic, halved
    ½ teaspoon each: Worcestershire sauce,
       Dijon prepared mustard, and prepared
       horseradish
    ½ teaspoon each: garlic salt and onion salt
       Coarse pepper to taste

Combine all ingredients in blender; whirl until smooth. Cover; chill at least an hour to blend flavors. Makes 2¼ cups. Excellent with all seafood salads.

GREEN BEAN AND TOMATO SALAD

(75 calories per serving)

For each serving, allow 1 medium tomato and all the cooked or canned green beans and crisp salad greens you wish. Peel tomato; slice or cut in wedges; arrange on greens; top with beans. Over all spoon 2 tablespoons Tangy Dressing (page 43) or 1½ tablespoons Green Onion Dressing (page 25).

BAKED WHOLE CHICKEN ROSEMARY

(serves 4 / 346 calories per serving)

> 1 (2½ to 3 lb.) whole chicken
> Seasoned salt and pepper to taste
> 1 teaspoon rosemary
> 1 large stalk celery, halved
> ½ medium onion, halved
> 1 clove garlic, halved
> 1 teaspoon chicken stock base
> ¼ cup hot water
> ¼ cup California Dry Vermouth

Reach in cavity of chicken and pull out any visible fat. Sprinkle cavity with salt, pepper, and some of the rosemary; stuff with celery, onion, and garlic. Twist wing tips and fold onto back so wings lie flat. Place chicken, breast up, in a baking dish with a tight-fitting lid; chicken should fit snugly. (There are special chicken-shaped cookers that do the job nicely, or you can use a Dutch oven or heavy casserole.) Dissolve chicken stock base in hot water; add wine; spoon over chicken. Sprinkle with salt, pepper, and remaining rosemary.

Cover; bake in 450° oven 1 hour. Remove chicken to a platter or carving board. Pour juices into a bowl; remove all possible fat. (A few ice cubes mixed into the juices will make fat solidify quickly for easy removal.) Reheat juices in a small saucepan; serve with the chicken. Size of portion: ½ breast; or leg and thigh.

CELERY HEARTS ROMANO

(serves 4 / 19 calories per serving)

Drain 1 (1 lb.) can celery hearts, reserving liquid. Place hearts, cut side up, in a shallow baking dish; pour in just enough celery liquid to cover bottom of dish. Sprinkle hearts with salt and pepper, then with 3 tablespoons grated Romano (or Parmesan) cheese; dust with paprika. Bake in 450° oven about 10 minutes, or until cheese melts and celery is thoroughly heated.

CASSEROLE MUSHROOMS

*(serves 4 / 8 calories per serving,
since mushrooms are an all-you-want vegetable)*

> ¾ pound medium-sized mushrooms
> 2 teaspoons chicken stock base
> ¼ cup hot water
> ¼ cup California White Table Wine
> 2 teaspoons lemon juice
> ½ teaspoon grated lemon peel
> 2 green onions, finely chopped
> Pinch each of thyme and marjoram
> Pepper to taste
> 2 tablespoons chopped parsley

Wipe mushrooms with a damp sponge or cloth; cut off stems flush with cap; place, cut side up, in shallow baking dish. Mix chicken stock base and water; add all remaining ingredients; spoon over mushrooms. Cover dish (use foil if it has no lid); bake in 450° oven 15 to 20 minutes, basting occasionally.

CUSTARD MONT BLANC

(serves 4 / 123 calories per serving)

> 4 egg whites
> ¼ cup sugar
> ⅛ teaspoon salt
> 1 teaspoon vanilla
> ¼ teaspoon almond extract
> ¼ teaspoon nutmeg
> ¾ cup evaporated skim milk
> ¾ cup water
> ¾ cup sliced fresh or calorie-reduced
>   canned peaches
> 2 tablespoons California Sweet Sherry

Beat egg whites with a fork just until well blended and slightly foamy. Add sugar, salt, vanilla, almond extract, and nutmeg; beat gently just until blended. Stir in milk and water. Pour into 4 custard cups; set in shallow pan; pour in hot tap water to depth of about 1 inch. Bake in 350° oven 50 to 60 minutes, until knife inserted near edge of custard comes out clean. Lift cups out of pan; cool on wire rack. Cover; refrigerate until serving time. To serve, run a small spatula around edge of custard to loosen; turn into dessert dish; top with peach slices. Spoon a little of the Sherry over each custard.

BREAKFAST
(200 calories)

Grapefruit Juice
*(½ cup fresh or canned unsweetened juice /
50 calories)*

Mushroom-Cheese Toast
*(spread 1 slice toast with 1 teaspoon anchovy
paste; cover with thinly sliced raw, cooked, or
canned mushrooms; top with a ¾ oz. slice process
American cheese; bake or broil to melt
cheese / 152 calories)*

Black Coffee or Tea

LUNCH
(300 calories)

Palace Chicken Salad*
or
Celery Salad Francisco*

Golden Toast Strips or Rye Wafers
(2 Strips, page 28, or 2 wafers / 42 calories)

Apricots
*(½ cup fresh or calorie-reduced canned
apricot halves / 43 calories)*

Black Coffee or Tea

DINNER
(550 calories)

Gazpacho*

Braised Stuffed Flank Steak*

Carrots
*(½ cup diced, cooked carrots, plus plenty of
chopped chives or parsley / 22 calories)*

Hominy Grits or Cornmeal
*(⅔ cup cooked grits or cornmeal; moisten with
the meat gravy / 82 calories)*

Ice Milk or Baked Applesauce Crisp
*(½ cup ice milk; or 1 serving Baked Applesauce
Crisp, page 32, with frozen dessert
topping / 142 calories)*

Wine Choice: California Chianti

Extra Foods for Non-Slimmers:

Breakfast: Broiled tomato

Lunch: Avocado slices with either salad; French roll

**Dinner: Shredded sharp Cheddar cheese stirred into
the grits or cornmeal; chocolate or butterscotch topping on the ice milk, or a scoop of
vanilla ice milk on Baked Applesauce Crisp**

The 1200-calorie figure includes 100 calories for the 4-ounce glass of dry Table Wine and 50 calories for the *all-you-want* vegetables as listed on page 14 and used in the menus and recipes. Recipes are included for all dishes marked with an asterisk.

PALACE CHICKEN SALAD

(serves 4 / 213 calories per serving)

1½ cups finely diced, cooked chicken
1 cup finely diced celery
1 tablespoon chopped capers
2 tablespoons chopped parsley
1 recipe (1½ cups) Anchovy-Tarragon
    Dressing (following)
    Salt to taste
    Lettuce, washed and chilled
    (all-you-want)
2 medium-sized tomatoes, peeled and
    chilled
1 (9 oz.) package frozen artichoke hearts,
    cooked, drained, and chilled
    Paprika and lemon pepper

Mix chicken, celery, capers, and parsley; stir in ½ cup Anchovy-Tarragon Dressing; season with salt, if needed. Press mixture firmly into 4 custard cups; chill thoroughly.

At serving time, line 4 salad or luncheon plates with shredded lettuce. Cut tomatoes crosswise in halves; place one half, cut side up, on each plate. Unmold chicken mixture on top of tomato; arrange artichoke hearts around the salad. Spoon remaining Anchovy-Tarragon Dressing (4 tablespoons per portion) over all; sprinkle with paprika and lemon pepper.

ANCHOVY-TARRAGON DRESSING

(12 calories per tablespoon, 198 per cup)

1¼ cups low-fat cottage cheese
¼ cup cultured buttermilk
1½ teaspoons California Dry Vermouth
1½ teaspoons California white wine
    tarragon vinegar
½ teaspoon lemon juice
1 teaspoon anchovy paste
2 green onions, sliced (include some
    green tops)
2 tablespoons snipped parsley sprigs
1 clove garlic, sliced
¾ teaspoon seasoned salt
¼ teaspoon each: Worcestershire sauce
    and dried tarragon
    Coarse pepper to taste

Combine all ingredients in a blender; whirl until smooth; cover; chill at least 1 hour to blend flavors. Makes 1½ cups. This is also excellent with any seafood salad.

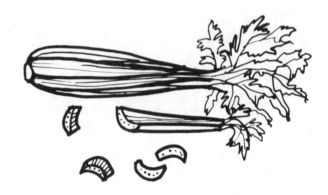

CELERY SALAD FRANCISCO

(serves 4 / 210 calories per serving)

2 good-sized heads celery
1 quart boiling water
4 teaspoons chicken stock base
2 cups cooked small shrimp, or 2 (4½ oz.)
    cans; or, 1⅓ cups cooked crabmeat, or
    1⅓ (7½ oz.) cans
1 recipe (¾ cup) White Wine Dressing
    (page 79)
    Lettuce, washed and chilled
    (all-you-want)
2 medium-sized tomatoes, peeled and
    chilled
    Whites of 2 hard-cooked eggs, shredded
8 anchovy fillets (rolled or flat)
    Paprika and lemon pepper

Wash heads of celery; trim base; cut off tops crosswise to make heads about 7 inches long. (Tops can be enjoyed raw or briefly cooked as an *all-you-want* vegetable.) Remove any very tough or disfigured stalks; use vegetable peeler if necessary to shave remaining coarse outer stalks; cut heads lengthwise in halves. Place, cut side up, in 12-inch skillet; add boiling water and chicken stock base. Cover; simmer about 12 minutes, or until celery is tender but still firm. Remove from heat; place celery in single layer in shallow baking dish; pour liquid over it. When cool, cover with foil or transparent wrap; chill several hours or overnight.

An hour or two before serving time, mix shrimp or crabmeat in a bowl with ¼ cup White Wine Dressing; cover; chill. At serving time, drain celery thoroughly on paper towels; place each half, cut side up, on lettuce-lined salad or luncheon plate; top with ½ cup marinated shrimp or ⅓ cup crabmeat, including any dressing marinade left in bowl. Cut tomatoes in sixths; place 3 wedges on each plate. Sprinkle some of the egg white over each salad; garnish with 2 anchovy fillets. Spoon remaining White Wine Dressing (2 tablespoons per portion) over salad; dust with paprika and lemon pepper.

GAZPACHO

(serves 8 / 43 calories per serving)

2 medium-sized tomatoes, peeled and
    quartered
¼ cup each: diced red Spanish onion and
    diced raw carrot
2 tablespoons each: diced, seeded
    cucumber and diced, seeded green
    pepper
  Few celery leaves
1 small clove garlic, sliced
2 cups tomato juice
2 cups vegetable juice cocktail
¼ cup California Dry Vermouth
1 tablespoon California red wine vinegar
  Salt and freshly ground black pepper
    to taste

Combine half of each vegetable in blender with 1 cup tomato juice and 1 cup vegetable juice cocktail; whirl just long enough to chop the vegetables but not too fine. Mixture should have texture, rather than be smooth. Pour into a large mixing bowl. Repeat process with remaining vegetables, tomato juice, and vegetable juice cocktail; add to first half in mixing bowl, stirring well. Add Vermouth, vinegar, salt, and pepper. Store, covered, in refrigerator several hours or, better still, overnight. Serve in chilled soup bowls, with or without an ice cube in each one. Makes 6 cups. *10 Carb/cup*
17 w/toast

BRAISED STUFFED FLANK STEAK

(serves 6 / 257 calories per serving)

1 flank steak (about 1½ lbs.)
1 (10 oz.) package frozen chopped
    spinach, cooked and very thoroughly
    drained
1 (4 oz.) can mushrooms stems and pieces,
    drained and chopped fine (reserve
    liquid)
3 tablespoons grated Parmesan cheese
1 egg white
4 tablespoons chopped parsley
1 clove garlic, chopped or pressed
¼ teaspoon mixed Italian seasoning
  Salt and pepper to taste
1 (10½ oz.) can condensed consommé
½ cup California Red Table Wine
1 carrot, sliced
1 large stalk celery, sliced
1 thick slice onion
½ bay leaf
3 whole allspice
  Dash each of thyme and marjoram
2 tablespoons instant-blending flour
1 (4 oz.) can sliced mushrooms, drained
    (reserve liquid)
1 tablespoon California Brandy
½ teaspoon Worcestershire sauce

Have meat dealer put steak through tenderizing machine. Mix spinach, chopped mushrooms, and Parmesan cheese. Stir egg white with fork just until it becomes slightly foamy; add to spinach mixture. Add 2 tablespoons parsley, chopped garlic, Italian seasoning, salt, and pepper; mix well. Spread mixture evenly over steak; roll up, from one wide side to the other, tucking in ends as you roll. Fasten steak roll with skewers or string. Place in Dutch oven or casserole with tight-fitting lid.

In saucepan, combine consommé, red wine, carrot, celery, onion, bay leaf, allspice, thyme, marjoram, and remaining 2 tablespoons parsley; bring to boil; pour over steak roll. Cover; bake in 350° oven 2 hours, or until meat is tender; turning and basting roll several times. Remove from oven; let meat cool to room temperature in liquid. Remove cooled meat from liquid; wrap in foil or place in covered casserole; refrigerate. Strain liquid into pint measuring pitcher, pressing pieces of vegetable with back of spoon to extract any juices; discard vegetables. Chill liquid several hours or overnight, until top layer of fat solidifies. (To hasten the process, set in the freezer.)

To make gravy: Remove layer of fat from chilled liquid; add enough reserved mushroom liquid (and water if needed) to make 1¾ cups. Mix ½ cup or so of this liquid with the flour; combine with remaining liquid in saucepan; stir over medium heat until mixture boils and thickens. Add sliced mushrooms, Brandy, and Worcestershire sauce; taste and correct seasoning.

To serve: With sharp knife, cut chilled steak roll crosswise in slices about ⅜-inch thick; heat slices briefly in the gravy. Size of portion: ⅙ of slices and approximately ⅓ cup gravy.

MENU
26
(1200 calories)

BREAKFAST
(200 calories)

Grapefruit
(½ medium grapefruit / 55 calories)

Scrambled Egg with Chili Pepper
(mix 1 egg with 1 tablespoon water and seasonings to taste; add 1 to 2 tablespoons chopped, seeded canned green chili peppers; scramble in ungreased Teflon pan; or, top scrambled egg with peppers before serving / 80 calories)

Toast
(1 slice / 65 calories)

Black Coffee or Tea

LUNCH
(300 calories)

Salad Plate:
Creamy Tomato Molds* with Shrimp or Crabmeat and Tangy Dressing
or
Bavarian Broccoli Mold* with Shrimp or Crabmeat and Tangy Dressing

Celery Hearts and Radishes
(all-you-want)

Golden Toast Strips or Rye Wafers
(4 Stripes, page 28, or 4 wafers / 84 calories)

Black Coffee or Tea

DINNER
(550 calories)

Artichoke-Caper Salad*
Stuffed Chicken Breasts Francine*

Chinese Pea Pods
(½ cup briefly cooked fresh or frozen Chinese pea pods / 20 calories)

Noodles
(½ cup cooked wide noodles lightly mixed with chopped parsley or chives to taste / 100 calories)

Lime Chiffon*

Gingersnaps or Vanilla Wafers
(2 small gingersnaps or wafers / 30 calories)

Wine Choice: California Rosé

Extra Foods for Non-Slimmers:

Breakfast: Vienna sausages

Lunch: Marinated garbanzos and pickled beets; strawberry sherbet

Dinner: Snipped anchovy fillets added to salad; Parmesan cheese on the noodles

The 1200-calorie figure includes 100 calories for the 4-ounce glass of dry Table Wine and 50 calories for the *all-you-want* vegetables as listed on page 14 and used in the menus and recipes. Recipes are included for all dishes marked with an asterisk.

CREAMY TOMATO MOLDS

(serves 4 / 55 calories per serving)

1 envelope unflavored gelatin
1 (12 oz.) can vegetable juice cocktail
¾ cup plain low-fat yoghurt
1 tablespoon California Dry Vermouth
1 tablespoon catsup
1 teaspoon California white wine vinegar
1 teaspoon grated green pepper
½ teaspoon grated onion
½ teaspoon Worcestershire sauce
Seasoned salt and pepper to taste

In a saucepan, sprinkle gelatin over ½ cup vegetable juice cocktail; stir over low heat 3 or 4 minutes, until gelatin dissolves. Remove from heat. Stir in remaining vegetable juice cocktail; add yoghurt and beat with wire whisk or fork until ingredients are smoothly blended; stir in remaining ingredients. Pour into 4 (½-cup) individual molds or custard cups that have been rinsed with cold water; chill until firm. Unmold on crisp salad greens *(all-you-want)*.

To complete Salad Plate:
Surround molds with cooked or canned small shrimp (¾ cup per portion) or flaked crabmeat (½ cup per portion). Serve with Tangy Dressing (page 43). Dressing portion for this salad: 2 tablespoons. Total calories for the Salad Plate: 211.

If you'd like to double this recipe to serve 8, you can mold it in a 5-cup (8½-inch) ring mold or 8 individual molds.

BAVARIAN BROCCOLI MOLD

(serves 6 / 55 calories per serving)

¼ cup California Dry Vermouth
¾ cup water
1 envelope unflavored gelatin
3 teaspoons (1 tablespoon) chicken stock base
1 cup plain low-fat yoghurt
1 teaspoon lemon juice
½ teaspoon Worcestershire sauce
Seasoned salt and pepper to taste
1 (10 oz.) package frozen chopped broccoli, cooked, drained, and chopped fine
Whites of 3 hard-cooked eggs, chopped or coarsely grated
1 tablespoon chopped pimiento
1 teaspoon grated onion

In a saucepan, combine wine and water; sprinkle in gelatin; stir over low heat 3 or 4 minutes, until gelatin is dissolved. Add chicken stock base; stir until dissolved. Remove from heat; cool 5 minutes or so. Add yoghurt, lemon juice, Worcestershire sauce, salt, and pepper; beat with wire whisk or fork until ingredients are well blended. Chill until mixture mounds slightly when dropped from tip of spoon; fold in remaining ingredients. Turn into a 1-quart ring mold that has been rinsed with cold water, or into 6 individual molds or custard cups; chill until firm. Unmold on crisp salad greens *(all-you-want)*.

To complete Salad Plate:
Fill center of ring, or surround individual molds, with cooked or canned small shrimp (¾ cup per portion) or flaked crabmeat (½ cup per portion). Serve with Tangy Dressing (page 43). Dressing portion for this salad: 2 tablespoons. Total calories for the Salad Plate: 211.

ARTICHOKE-CAPER SALAD

(serves 6 / 39 calories per serving)

2 (9 oz.) packages frozen artichoke hearts
½ cup Tangy Dressing (page 43)
2 tablespoons drained capers
2 tablespoons chopped parsley

Cook artichoke hearts according to package directions. Drain thoroughly; while still warm, combine with other ingredients, mixing lightly. Cover; chill several hours or, better still, overnight. Serve on crisp lettuce *(all-you-want)*.

STUFFED CHICKEN BREASTS FRANCINE

(serves 6 / 255 calories per serving)

Have your meat dealer bone and halve 3 (approx. 10 oz.) chicken breasts. Remove skin; put each piece of chicken between two sheets of waxed paper; pound until flattened. Spread each piece with Spinach-Mushroom Stuffing (following); roll sides in toward center to keep stuffing from escaping, then roll up from top to bottom. Place, seam down, in shallow baking pan; sprinkle with salt, pepper, and paprika. Chill thoroughly (at least 1 hour). Pour in just enough water to cover bottom of pan; cover chicken loosely with foil; bake in 350° oven 1 hour. Remove from oven. If dish is not to be finished at once, cool chicken in liquid; cover tightly with foil; refrigerate. Before serving, place chicken in Mushroom Sauce (following); heat gently but thoroughly. To serve, place chicken on heated dinner plates; spoon sauce over each breast. (There will be about 6 tablespoons sauce per portion.)

Spinach-Mushroom Stuffing:
½ pound fresh mushrooms
¼ cup California Medium Sherry
½ cup chopped, cooked spinach
3 tablespoons canned chicken spread
   (half of a 4¾ oz. can)
½ teaspoon grated onion
½ teaspoon Worcestershire sauce
   Pinch each of thyme and rosemary
   Seasoned salt and pepper to taste

Wipe mushrooms with damp cloth or sponge; remove tough portion of stems; chop mushrooms fairly fine. Combine mushrooms and Sherry in skillet; cover; simmer gently 5 minutes, shaking pan frequently. Remove cover; continue cooking until any liquid is evaporated. Mix mushrooms with all remaining ingredients, blending thoroughly. Spread over chicken breasts as directed.

Mushroom Sauce:
½ pound fresh mushrooms
1 tablespoon diet margarine
2 tablespoons chopped onion
3 tablespoons instant-blending flour
1½ cups canned chicken broth
   (not condensed)
½ cup California White Table Wine
2 tablespoons chopped parsley
1 tablespoon California Medium Sherry
½ teaspoon Worcestershire sauce
   Dash of thyme
   Seasoned salt and pepper to taste

Wipe mushrooms with damp cloth or sponge; remove tough portion of stems; slice mushrooms thin. Melt margarine in 10-inch Teflon skillet; add mushrooms and onion; sauté, uncovered, over medium heat 5 minutes, stirring often. Blend flour and chicken broth; add to mushrooms; add white wine; stir over medium heat until mixture boils and thickens. Add remaining ingredients. Heat chicken breasts in sauce as directed.

LIME CHIFFON

(serves 8 / 90 calories per serving)

⅔ cup cold water
⅓ cup California Muscatel
2 envelopes unflavored gelatin
¼ cup sugar
⅛ teaspoon salt
1 (6 oz.) can frozen limeade concentrate
   (keep frozen)
½ cup ice water
2 egg whites

Combine cold water and wine in small saucepan; sprinkle in gelatin; stir over low heat 2 to 3 minutes, until gelatin is completely dissolved. Stir in sugar and salt. Add frozen limeade concentrate and ice water; stir until limeade melts. Chill until slightly thicker than consistency of unbeaten egg white. Add egg whites to gelatin mixture; beat until mixture begins to hold its shape. Turn into a 6-cup mold; chill until firm. Unmold; garnish, if desired, with a slice of lime or a sprig of mint (no extra calories). When serving, top each portion with 1 tablespoon frozen whipped dessert topping (16 calories).

If you prefer, you can spoon the mixture into 8 dessert dishes instead of a mold. At serving time, top each portion with 1 tablespoon frozen whipped dessert topping and garnish with a slice of lime or a sprig of mint.

MENU 27

(1200 calories)

BREAKFAST
(200 calories)

Strawberries or Orange Juice
*(1 cup capped fresh or unsweetened frozen berries
or ½ cup orange juice / 55 calories)*

Liver Pâté on Rye Wafers or Toast
*(2 tablespoons canned pâté with 3 wafers or 1
slice toast / 147 calories)*

Black Coffee or Tea

LUNCH
(300 calories)

Zucchini-Stuffed Peppers*
and
Toast or Rye Wafers
*(1 slice toast or 3 wafers with 1 teaspoon diet
margarine / 82 calories)*
or
Baked Tomato Sandwich Parmigiana*

Asparagus Salad
*(6 spears chilled asparagus on lettuce with 1
tablespoon Tangy Dressing (page 43) / 46 calories)*

Apple or Applesauce
*(1 medium apple; or ½ cup unsweetened apple-
sauce mixed with 1½ teaspoons sugar and
cinnamon to taste / 75 calories)*

Black Coffee or Tea

DINNER
(550 calories)

Mushroom Cocktail*

Poached Halibut Steaks*
served hot with Golden Sauce*
or
**served cold with Anchovy Sauce, Caper Sauce,
or Yoghurt Tartar Sauce**
or
Barbecued or Broiled Halibut Steaks*
Curried Spinach Purée*

Carrots or Beets
*(½ cup cooked, diced carrots or beets /
30 calories)*

Sherried Chocolate Pear*

Vanilla Wafers or Gingersnaps
(2 wafers or small gingersnaps / 30 calories)

Wine Choice: California Riesling

Extra Foods for Non-Slimmers:

Breakfast: Crisp bacon

Lunch: Brownie with the apple or applesauce

**Dinner: Frozen French-fried or canned shoestring
potatoes; top pear with a scoop of vanilla ice
milk then spoon on Sherry and chocolate sauce**

The 1200-calorie figure includes 100 calories for the 4-ounce glass of dry Table Wine and 50 calories for the *all-you-want* vegetables as listed on page 14 and used in the menus and recipes. Recipes are included for all dishes marked with an asterisk.

BAKED TOMATO SANDWICH PARMIGIANA

(serves 3 / 175 calories per serving)

½ cup plain low-fat yoghurt
⅓ cup grated Parmesan cheese
1½ teaspoons California Dry Vermouth
½ teaspoon prepared mustard
¼ teaspoon Worcestershire sauce
1 tablespoon finely chopped green onion
  (include some green top)
  Seasoned salt and pepper to taste
3 slices bread
2 medium tomatoes, peeled and thinly
  sliced
  Paprika
2 tablespoons bacon-flavored bits

In small mixing bowl blend yoghurt, cheese, Vermouth, mustard, and Worcestershire sauce; stir in onion, salt, and pepper. (Easy on the salt; the bacon bits will contribute some.) Toast bread slices on one side; cover untoasted side with slices of tomato, cutting tomato as necessary to fit neatly. Spread Parmesan mixture evenly over tomatoes; sprinkle with paprika. Place sandwiches on baking sheet; bake in 450° oven about 10 minutes, or until topping is lightly browned. If desired, place under broiler a minute to finish browning.

To serve, cut sandwiches in half; place on luncheon plates; sprinkle with bacon bits. A bit of greenery (parsley or watercress sprigs, or a frilly lettuce leaf) will add color but not calories to the plate.

MUSHROOM COCKTAIL

(serves 3 / 40 calories per serving)

In small bowl, mix 3 tablespoons each catsup and chili sauce, 1 tablespoon each California Dry Vermouth and lemon juice, and ¼ teaspoon each prepared horseradish and Worcestershire sauce. Cover; chill an hour or more. Shortly before serving time, line 3 sherbet glasses or other suitable dishes with crisp lettuce. Wipe 6 (2-inch) mushrooms clean; remove tough portion of stems; slice mushrooms thin. Divide mushrooms among the 3 dishes; spoon chilled sauce over each portion. Sprinkle with chopped chives or parsley.

ZUCCHINI-STUFFED PEPPERS

(serves 4 / 95 calories per serving)

2 medium-sized green peppers
1 (1 lb.) can zucchini in tomato sauce
1 (4 oz.) can mushroom stems and pieces,
  drained
2 egg whites
½ cup shredded Cheddar cheese
2 tablespoons chopped parsley
1 tablespoon chopped green onion
  Chopped or pressed garlic or garlic salt
  to taste
  Seasoned salt and pepper to taste
4 teaspoons grated Parmesan cheese
2 tablespoons California Dry Vermouth
  Pinch of oregano

Cut peppers lengthwise in halves; remove seeds and tough white membrane. Place pepper halves in saucepan; cover with boiling water; boil 5 minutes; drain. Empty can of zucchini into a strainer set over a bowl; drain as much sauce as possible from zucchini by pressing gently with rubber spatula or back of spoon. Set sauce aside. Chop zucchini and mushrooms together just until coarsely diced. Stir egg whites with a fork just until well blended and only slightly foamy; add zucchini-mushroom mixture; mix well. Add Cheddar cheese, parsley, onion, garlic, salt, and pepper. Place pepper halves in a 9-inch pie plate; fill with zucchini mixture; sprinkle each half with 1 teaspoon Parmesan cheese. (If peppers are inclined to be ''loppy,'' gently push them close together so they rest against each other.) Mix reserved tomato sauce, Vermouth, and oregano; spoon around (not over) filled peppers. Bake in 375° oven 30 to 35 minutes, until sauce is bubbly and filling is firm. Remove from oven; let settle a few minutes before serving. Serves 4.

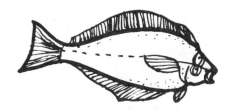

POACHED HALIBUT STEAKS

(serves 3 / 237 calories per serving)

1¼ pounds halibut steaks (3 steaks)
1 cup California White Table Wine
2 or 3 slices onion
1 teaspoon whole mixed pickling spice
1 teaspoon salt

Place fish in single layer in skillet; add remaining ingredients. Pour in just enough boiling water so fish is barely covered; cover skillet; simmer very, very gently about 10 minutes, or just until fish is tender.

To serve hot: Lift steaks onto warm dinner plates with slotted spatula so they will be well drained; garnish with sprigs of watercress or parsley (no added calories). Serve with Golden Sauce (below). Sauce portion for this menu: ⅓ cup / 60 calories.

To serve cold: Remove cooked steaks from liquid; reserve liquid. Place steaks in a shallow dish; let cool, then pour liquid over them. Cover (with foil if the dish has no lid); chill. At serving time, drain steaks thoroughly on paper towels; place on dinner plates. Garnish each portion with sprigs of watercress or parsley and ½ medium tomato, peeled and sliced or cut in wedges (16 calories). Serve with Anchovy Sauce, Caper Sauce, or Yoghurt Tartar Sauce (page 26). Sauce portion for this menu: 3 tablespoons / 27 calories.

GOLDEN SAUCE

(11 calories per tablespoon, 176 per cup)

1 cup plain low-fat yoghurt
1 tablespoon diet margarine
1 teaspoon prepared mustard (the yellow variety)
1½ teaspoons California Dry Vermouth
1 teaspoon lemon juice
Generous dash of lemon pepper
Garlic salt and/or onion salt to taste

Combine all ingredients in top of small double boiler; stir over hot (not boiling) water just until margarine melts and sauce is warm. Do not heat too fast or too long or sauce will curdle! The ingredients can be combined ahead of time, but don't heat until just before serving. Makes 1 cup.

BARBECUED OR BROILED HALIBUT STEAKS

(serves 3 / 293 calories per serving)

1¼ pounds halibut steaks (3 steaks)
⅓ cup California Dry Vermouth
3 tablespoons soy sauce
1 tablespoon vegetable salad oil
1 tablespoon lemon juice
1 green onion, thinly sliced
1 tablespoon chopped parsley
1 small clove garlic, chopped or pressed
Pinch of thyme

Place fish in single layer in a shallow dish; mix remaining ingredients; pour over fish. Cover with foil or transparent wrap; refrigerate several hours, turning fish occasionally. Cook on the barbecue or broil in the oven, basting with the marinade. Serve with lemon wedges *(all-you-want)*.

CURRIED SPINACH PURÉE

(serves 3 / 62 calories per serving)

1 (10 oz.) package frozen chopped spinach
2 tablespoons instant minced onion
1 small clove garlic
¼ cup powdered non-fat milk
¼ teaspoon curry powder (or more to taste)
½ cup cold water
Seasoned salt and pepper to taste

Cook spinach according to package directions just until thoroughly thawed; drain well by putting in strainer and pressing out liquid with rubber spatula or back or spoon. Combine spinach in blender with all remaining ingredients except salt and pepper; whirl until smooth. Turn mixture into a saucepan. Just before serving, heat gently until piping hot; season to taste.

SHERRIED CHOCOLATE PEAR

(91 calories per serving)

For each serving, allow half of a medium-sized fresh pear, or ½ cup fresh or calorie-reduced canned pear slices; 1 teaspoon California Medium Sherry; 1 tablespoon canned chocolate syrup. Put pear in dessert dish; spoon on Sherry, then chocolate syrup. An interesting and delightful combination of flavors.

MENU

28

(1200 calories)

BREAKFAST
(200 calories)

Sliced Banana with Cereal
*(½ large banana, sliced, with 1 cup unsweetened
corn flakes or wheat flakes cereal, ½ cup
non-fat milk, and non-caloric sweetener to
taste / 202 calories)*

Black Coffee or Tea

LUNCH
(300 calories)

Antipasto*
Zucchini Verde*

Mozzarella Cheese
(1-ounce slice / 84 calories)

Rye Wafers or Saltines
(3 wafers or 5 saltines / 63 calories)

Black Coffee or Tea

DINNER
(550 calories)

Tossed Green Salad
*(for each serving, allow ½ medium tomato and
1 tablespoon Tangy Dressing (page 43) plus all
the sliced cucumbers, sliced radishes, and crisp
greens you want / 37 calories)*

Dilly Beef Rolls* or Swiss Pepper Steak*

Green Beans or Crookneck Squash
(all-you-want vegetables)

Baked Potato
*(1 medium, 3-to-a-lb.; fluff up and
moisten with gravy from the meat; omit skin /
92 calories)*

Nectar Rosé
*(page 26; top with frozen whipped dessert
topping as directed in recipe / 118 calories)*

Wine Choice: California Claret

Extra Foods for Non-Slimmers:

Breakfast: Raisin bread toast

Lunch: Marinated garbanzos; Swiss and / or Monterey
Jack cheese; thinly sliced pastrami, corned beef,
or chipped beef (all available packaged); grapes
or papaya

Dinner: Seasoned croutons (packaged) added to the
salad; sour half and half on the baked potato;
macaroons with Nectar Rosé

The 1200-calorie figure includes 100 calories for the 4-ounce glass of dry Table Wine and 50 calories for the *all-you-want* vegetables as listed on page 14 and used in the menus and recipes. Recipes are included for all dishes marked with an asterisk.

ANTIPASTO
(serves 8 / 127 calories per serving)

- 1½ cups small cauliflowerets
- 1 cup sliced carrots
- 1 cup cut green beans
- 1 teaspoon whole mixed pickling spice
- 2 tablespoons California white wine vinegar
  Salt to taste
- 2 (8 oz.) cans tomato sauce
- ½ cup California Dry Vermouth
- 2 tablespoons California red wine vinegar
- 1 (2 oz.) can anchovy fillets, well drained on a paper towel and cut fine
- 1 large clove garlic, chopped or pressed
- 1 tablespoon Worcestershire sauce
  Generous dash of lemon pepper
- 1 (3½ oz.) jar tiny whole cocktail onions, plus 1 tablespoon of the juice
- 6 tiny (approx. 2½-in.) dill pickles, sliced, plus 1 tablespoon of the juice
- 2 (6½ oz.) cans diet-pack tuna, drained and flaked
- 1 (14 oz.) can artichoke hearts, drained, rinsed, and cut in halves or thirds
- 1 (8 oz.) can whole mushrooms, drained
- 1 (3½ oz.) jar capers, drained
- 1 (3¼ oz.) jar small pimiento-stuffed olives, drained
- 1 (2 oz.) jar sliced pimientos, drained

In 10-inch skillet, combine cauliflowerets, carrots, and green beans; add pickling spice, white wine vinegar, and salt. Pour in about 1 inch boiling water; cover; simmer 10 minutes, or until vegetables are tender but still firm. Drain; discard spices; let vegetables cool. In saucepan, combine tomato sauce, Vermouth, red wine vinegar, anchovies, garlic, Worcestershire sauce, and lemon pepper; heat to simmering; cook gently 2 or 3 minutes, stirring to dissolve anchovies. Remove from heat; stir in the 1 tablespoon juice from cocktail onions and dill pickles; taste and add salt, if needed.

In a shallow baking dish (8 by 12 by 2 inches) arrange half of all the solid ingredients (cooked vegetables, drained cocktail onions, sliced dill pickles, tuna, artichoke hearts, mushrooms, capers, olives, and pimientos). Scatter ingredients evenly over bottom of dish so that when *Antipasto* is served, it will be easy to scoop up some of everything for each person. Spoon half of tomato sauce mixture over all. Repeat with remaining solid ingredients and sauce; shake dish gently to level ingredients. Cover dish tightly with foil; chill overnight, or for at least 4 or 5 hours. From time to time, tilt dish gently and baste ingredients with the sauce. (A bulb-type turkey baster is very handy here.)

To serve, use a spatula and a spoon; lift solid ingredients onto lettuce-lined plates with the spatula; spoon some of the sauce over each portion.

ZUCCHINI VERDE
(serves 8 / 22 calories per serving)

- 1½ pounds small zucchini
- 1 teaspoon chicken stock base
- ⅓ cup hot water
- ⅓ cup California Dry Vermouth
- 3 tablespoons California white wine tarragon vinegar
- 1 tablespoon vegetable salad oil
- 4 anchovy fillets, drained on a paper towel and cut fine
- 1 clove garlic, chopped or pressed
- ½ teaspoon each: seasoned salt and coarse pepper
- ¼ teaspoon each: garlic salt, celery salt, and oregano
- ¼ cup chopped parsley

Wash zucchini and trim off ends; slice crosswise very thin; turn into a 10-inch Teflon skillet. Dissolve chicken stock base in hot water; add to zucchini. Stir over medium-high heat until mixture is steamy; cover, turn heat low, and cook, stirring frequently, 5 to 7 minutes, or just until zucchini is tender but still firm. Remove from heat; drain zucchini; place in a shallow casserole. Mix remaining ingredients; pour over zucchini; stir gently to coat pieces of zucchini with the mixture. Cover, using foil if the dish has no lid of its own; chill overnight, or at least 6 to 8 hours, stirring occasionally. Serve in crisp lettuce cups or on a bed of watercress. (No added calories to count, since greens are an *all-you-want* vegetable.) Be sure to spoon a little of the juice over each serving.

DILLY BEEF ROLLS

(serves 4 / 299 calories per serving)

½   pound fresh mushrooms
1¼ pounds round steak (as lean as possible),
      cut ½ inch thick
1   dill pickle, quartered lengthwise
2   tablespoons diet margarine
1   tablespoon tomato paste
1   teaspoon beef stock base
½   cup hot water
½   cup California Red Table Wine
2   tablespoons chopped onion
2   tablespoons chopped parsley
1   clove garlic, chopped or pressed
      Dash each of thyme and marjoram
      Salt and pepper to taste
1   tablespoon instant-blending flour
1   tablespoon California Dry Sherry

Wipe mushrooms with damp cloth or sponge; remove tough portion of stems; slice mushrooms thin; set aside. Trim any fat and skin from meat. Using a meat tenderizer, mallet, or edge of a heavy plate, pound meat to ¼-inch thickness; cut in 4 pieces as nearly uniform as possible. Roll each piece around a pickle quarter; secure with skewers or tie with string. Melt margarine in 10-inch Teflon skillet; brown meat rolls nicely on all sides. Add tomato paste and beef stock base to hot water; stir until blended; pour over meat. Add red wine, mushrooms, onion, parsley, garlic, and seasonings. Cover; simmer gently 1 to 1½ hours, or until meat is very tender, turning and basting rolls occasionally.

Remove meat and mushrooms from skillet; pull out skewers or cut string. Measure liquid; add water to make 1⅓ cups; pour back into skillet. Blend flour with ⅓ cup cold water; stir into liquid in skillet; cook, stirring, over medium heat until mixture boils. Add Sherry; taste and correct seasoning as needed. Return meat and mushrooms to pan; cover; heat very gently for a few minutes before serving.

SWISS PEPPER STEAK

(serves 4 / 296 calories per serving)

½   pound fresh mushrooms
1¼ pounds round steak (as lean as possible),
      cut ½ inch thick
1   tablespoon plus 1 teaspoon instant-
      blending flour
1   tablespoon diet margarine
1   teaspoon beef stock base
½   cup hot water
¼   cup California White Table Wine
1   green pepper, slivered
1   tomato, peeled and cut in eighths
¼   cup chopped onion
1   clove garlic, chopped or pressed
      Dash each of thyme and marjoram
      Seasoned salt and pepper to taste
2   tablespoons California Dry Vermouth

Wipe mushrooms with damp cloth or sponge; remove tough portion of stems; slice mushrooms thin; set aside. Trim any fat and skin from meat. Using a meat tenderizer, mallet, or edge of heavy plate, pound meat to ¼-inch thickness; cut across grain into strips about ¾ inch wide. Put meat strips in a paper bag with 1 tablespoon of the flour; shake to coat strips with flour. Melt margarine in 10-inch Teflon skillet; brown meat strips nicely on both sides. Dissolve beef stock base in hot water; pour over meat. Add white wine, mushrooms, green pepper, tomato, onion, garlic, and seasonings. Cover; simmer gently 1 hour or longer, until meat is tender, stirring frequently. Blend remaining 1 teaspoon flour with Vermouth; stir into sauce; simmer a minute or so. Before serving, taste and correct seasoning if necessary.

Wine at Home
Its Care, Storage, Service
Refrigeration and Bottling

It is obvious that if there is only one dieter in a household, it will take him or her at least six days to consume one bottle (one-fifth gallon or 25.6 ounces) of table wine at the ration recommended in this book of one four-ounce glass at dinner. Also wine is used as a cooking ingredient in many of the four week's recipes, requiring that several wines be kept on hand. Therefore, advice on how to care for wines properly in the home will be valuable in the particular situation of the slimmer, as well as for the general purposes of host and hostess, and all-around wine enthusiast.

Table wines are subject to decline after prolonged exposure to air, as are many other foods and beverages. Once they are opened, it is best to use such wines—Burgundy, Cabernet Sauvignon, Rosé, Rhine Wine, Riesling, etc.—within a few days for fullest taste satisfaction, even though the bottle is recapped or recorked and placed in the refrigerator.

However, if handled with care and exposure to the air is kept to a minimum, table wines in half-gallon and gallon jugs are an excellent buy and may be decanted (poured gently) after opening into smaller bottles for longer storage, whether in or out of the refrigerator. Also, for convenience, a carafe or decanter may be filled from the jug for table service.

Bottles of wine with screw caps of both one-fifth gallon and one-tenth gallon (12.8 ounces) sizes may be purchased from your local retailer and these bottles saved when empty for rebottling wines from larger containers.

All bottles should be thoroughly washed, rinsed and sterilized with hot water before they are utilized for rebottling purposes. If original wine bottle corks are reused, be sure they do not leak when partially consumed bottles are laid on their sides. Screw cap bottles may be kept upright, but they too should be tightly closed.

Thoroughly clean soft drink or soda water bottles with screw caps are another good home bottling answer to storing diet rations, eliminating the necessity of opening the larger container every day. Fill one inch to one-and-a-half inches from the top, keeping air at a minimum but allowing a little room for expansion of the wine.

Of course you are going to want to celebrate the disappearance of that first five or ten pounds, after having faithfully adhered to the menus and recipes in this book. The nicest way to do this is with a bottle of delicious California Champagne. Select the driest—either Natural or Brut—and enjoy a glassful of tingling, bracing wine, knowing that it will not overturn your diet regimen.

Remember that all sparkling wines are at their best when served thoroughly chilled and consumed immediately after opening. So share your celebration bottle with family or friends, as storage of a once-opened bottle is very likely to cause it to lose its sparkling zestiness.

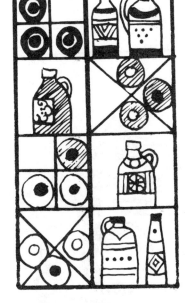

Dessert or appetizer wines such as Port, Sherry, Dry or Sweet Vermouth, Muscatel and Tokay, because of their higher alcohol content, ranging between 17 and 21 percent, will generally keep for two to three months after opening, without refrigeration. However, bottles of these wines should be tightly closed after each use and kept in a cool, dry place. Again, corked bottles should rest on their sides, bottles with screw cap closure standing upright.

It is also a good idea to buy your wine by the case to take advantage of case lot discounts often available to retail outlets. Even though all California wines are ready to be enjoyed at the time of purchase, some enophiles prefer to age them longer at home. This is particularly true of red table wines, as some types do continue to improve with extended bottle aging. White table wines and rosés are generally bottled at the winery when fairly young and fruity—as they should be—and do not derive the same benefits from further aging in the bottle as do some reds.

Experienced wine merchants will gladly give advice on which wines will significantly improve from additional aging in your own home.

The Wine Cellar at Home

Since the main sources of harm to wine are sunlight, rapid temperature changes and vibration, the logical place to keep your wines is a cool, dark basement, away from furnace, washing machine, etc. Lacking a basement, a broom closet will do admirably, but keep in mind that it should be on an inside wall or in a northern exposure where the temperature is lowest with minimal variation. Wine stores best at temperatures less than 70°.

Bottles of wine closed with plastic-lined screw caps, or plastic stoppers (as are many California Champagnes), can be stored either standing upright or lying down. Corked bottles should always be placed on their sides to keep the cork moist from contact with the wine. If the cork is allowed to dry out, it will eventually shrink and permit air seepage to the liquid, and this will cause spoilage.

Since temperatures at floor level are coolest, white wines and sparkling wines should be stored lowest, then red wines at mid-level and dessert and appetizer wines at the top.

White wines and Champagnes are made under cool conditions at the winery, and are best when served chilled. Keeping them at floor level not only suits them as a matter of storage, it shortens the chilling time when you want to serve them. Reds are fermented at higher temperatures and seem to be enjoyed most when served at cool room temperatures of less than 70°.

The appetizer and dessert wines are aged in warm rooms and are not in the least injured by being stored in the warmest part of the home wine cellar, nearest the ceiling.

Racks, bins or cabinets to hold your wines can be home-built, commercially manufactured, simple and inexpensive, or elaborate and expensive—and tailored to whatever your needs may be.

The simplest solution of all is to obtain from your retailer one of those sturdy cardboard cartons in which wines come packed, turn it on its side on the floor of a suitable closet or cabinet and store cork-stoppered bottles in it, horizontally. As your cellar grows, your accommodations can be expanded. It's amazing how, after a bottle or two of wine have made themselves at home, you will decide to make room for more until your personal wine cellar has become a permanent household institution.

Plain and Fancy Wine Service

Your glass of wine at dinner can be simply poured in the kitchen and put on the table when food is served, or, if the ritual pleases you, you can serve wine this way:

First, if it is a red wine, you may want to open it an hour early, to let it "breathe" and develop its aroma and flavor potential. Pull the cork gently, taking care not to disturb the wine. If the wine is white or rosé, you can dramatize its service and accomplish the useful purpose of maintaining its chill too, by placing it in a bucket of ice beside the table, with a napkin handy.

If there are guests, the host may want to pour a bit of wine first into his own glass to sniff and sip, to make sure it is pleasing to the taste. Then, the ladies' glasses are filled first, clockwise, around the table, and gentlemen are served counterclockwise. The host's glass is filled last and he can relax—providing there is enough wine to go around. Remember to allow a minimum of one bottle (26.5 ounces) for each four guests.

Or this ritual can be dispensed with by simply passing the bottle or decanter around the table and letting your guests help themselves. The main objective is to enjoy the wine.

As with most wine lore, there is tradition connected with serving temperatures of wine, which can be observed or ignored, usually with equally happy results. Red wines, as a case in point, are traditionally served at room temperature; but that custom came to us from England where rooms are a good deal cooler than today's modern American home. Perhaps "cellar temperature" would be a more accurate description—between 60° and 70°. In any event some people prefer their red wines briefly chilled in the refrigerator, others prefer them at room or at cellar temperature.

Rosé and white wines, on the other hand, are considered most enjoyable when chilled to about 50°. An hour in the refrigerator should take care of this. However Champagne and other sparkling wines are served thoroughly chilled—almost everyone seems to agree on this—but not below 35°. Three to four hours in the refrigerator should do the job.

Appetizer and dessert wines may be served at room temperature, but many people prefer them slightly chilled or even "on the rocks."

Special Natural Wines, which are pure grape wines flavored with natural fruit juices or essences, are considered to be at their tastiest best when served chilled.

One thing can be counted on. Chilled or not, wine will bring many pleasurable moments to dieter and non-dieter alike. High in nutritive value, economical in calories, with color to bewitch the eye and flavors to suit any palate, California wines are perfect companions, at mealtime or any other occasion.

With this book at hand and wine on the shelf, you are now ready to eat, drink and be merry, *even* while dieting!

WINE CALORIE CHART

Wine	Calories per Oz.	Oz. per Serving	Food Combinations
Red Table Wines	**24 to 25**	**4**	Most preferred with steaks, roasts, game, spaghetti, cheeses, stews, casseroles. See menus 3, 15, 28.
White Table Wines	**22 to 26**	**4**	Most preferred with fish, shellfish, poultry. See menus 11, 17, 24.
Champagnes and Other Sparkling Wines	**24 to 25**	**3**	These festive wines are appropriate anytime, along with food or by themselves.
Dry Sherry	**33***	**3**	Usually drunk before meals or with soup course.
Dessert Wines	**41 to 45****	**3**	Particularly good with fruit, nuts, cheese, plain cake, cookies.

*33 calories when label states 17% alcohol, 38 calories when 20% alcohol.

**41 to 45 calories when label states 18% alcohol, 44 to 48 when 20% alcohol.

More on Wine, Health and Dieting

Successful Experiments

In 1952 Dr. Giorgio Lolli of the International Center for Psychodietetics in Rome and New York City, and his associates, analyzed the diets of native-born Italians and Italian-Americans to find that the ingestion of quickly absorbable carbohydrates, such as pastries and candies, was appreciably lower among Italians who regularly consume wine with meals, than among their counterparts in the United States, who have drifted away from regular use of wine.

Following this he conducted a prolonged experiment with twenty-seven over-weight volunteers. First they dieted without wine, and then wine was introduced in three different ways; half an hour to an hour *before* dinner; *with* dinner; or half an hour to an hour *after* dinner. When wine was served during dinner, twenty-two of the subjects lost weight each week. When wine was served either before or after dinner, the results were less favorable, although some individuals did lose weight in each case.

Dr. Lolli, also noted how well wine was able to reduce tensions. Subjects suffering from fatigue and anxiety were often relieved of their discomfort by taking wine with their meal. Of course, emotional relief was especially noticeable in those subjects who were losing the greatest amount of weight.

On occasion, loss of weight was exceptionally marked. One woman began the test diet weighing 180 pounds, and at the end of the study she weighed 134 pounds. Taking the wine *after* dinner enabled her to lose an average of 2.4 pounds per week. Approximately 120 calories of wine per day (about five ounces) were needed to reduce her total caloric intake from an average of 3,250 calories before the program to 2,200 calories during the program. After the experiment had ended, she maintained her weight loss by taking a glass of wine, instead of nibbling, whenever she felt particularly fatigued or hungry.

Another subject, a 200-pound, 5'9" man, reduced his weight to 165 pounds by taking wine *with* his dinner.

The subjects chose any type of wine they wished, from dry wine to dessert wine; no important differences were ascribed to the various wine-types selected. Each subject consumed from four to five ounces of wine per day.

Eight subjects took wine only at bedtime; they were the nocturnal refrigerator raiders. Wine helped five of them to reduce their midnight raids appreciably. Even backsliders did not gain any more weight and some even lost weight slightly.

This study proved that taking wine with dinner automatically reduces the intake of calories from carbohydrates.

When our gastric juices are stimulated by hunger or appetite and signal to us that it is time to eat, our senses of taste and smell become more acute and weaken after satiation. Yet, unfortunately, the satisfaction of appetite is not governed solely by an amount of food and drink sufficient to meet the real needs of the body. This is illustrated nicely by the old saying, "Your eyes are bigger than your stomach."

It should therefore be of real interest to the dieter that the brain can be trained to alter its appetite satisfaction system through careful food selection and timing of the elements of a meal. By paying some attention to the mechanics of appetite, the amount of food eaten can be altered with little psychological discomfort to the dieter.

Wine and Appetite

Foods which cause appetite to become either sharper or duller are the keys to a diet, especially if one's appetite tends to get out of step with one's nutritional needs. Wine, in its great variety, can offer sweetness or tartness, or both combined. The acids lend a faint tartness to many wines and serve to stimulate the appetite; residual sugar, if any, can diminish it. Alcohol can also lessen the appetite. The net effect of wine depends largely on when it is taken—whether before the meal, or with it, and in what quantity.

Wine as a weight-reducing agent should be consumed with the meal rather than before it and considered as a one-for-one replacement of some other food calories, which ideally should come from carbohydrates. The wine has to be both dry and relatively low in organic acids, so as to minimize both calorie intake and appetite stimulation. Dry Sherries and aged dry wines are rich and filling, due to the intensity of their flavors, and both have the appropriate chemical make-up. The successful dieter thus is likely to wind up a wine connoisseur as well as slim and trim!

Of course to lose a large amount of weight and keep it lost, strict adherence to a low-calorie diet is essential. Such a diet puts additional physical and mental strain upon those who are already under stress, and even those dieters who are relatively free from anxiety are apt to lose patience with their rigorous and seemingly endless dietetic routine.

Wine is far more effective in the reducing diet than tablets designed to diminish appetite.

As my colleague, Dr. Robert C. Stepto, said at a recent Symposium on Wine and Health, "Our experience with wine is a few thousand years older than with artificial tranquilizers. Its safety is known, its freedom from side effects is certainly an advantage, as is the fact that wine is far more natural and economical than pills."

And at the same gathering, another prominent physician, Dr. William Dock, added these words of comfort to the prospective dieter: "When you add alcohol to a diet low in calories as well as in animal fats and salt, you make the diet much more acceptable to the patient. He will adhere more to his regimen than he would to a diet without wine."

With the help of wine and the menus and recipes in this book, you may perform a successful experiment of your own in weight loss. One word of caution, however, reiterating Emily Chase's recommendation, check with your own doctor before embarking on any diet program and follow his or her advice.

Aldehydes, Acids, Esters, and Polyphenols

Some of the aldehydes in wine seem to exert a therapeutic effect; some contribute to the flavor of a wine, even though they are present in the minutest quantity. As a whole, the organic acids in wine help to stimulate the appetite by encouraging the secretion of gastric juice in the stomach, as well as in the intestines. Most of these acids are ultimately converted into body protein; some, especially lactic acid, exhibit antibacterial action.

The acidity of wine resembles that of human gastric juice more closely than that of any other beverage, and it is essentially the relatively high acidity that allows wine to be easily assimilated.

Esters contribute rather gloriously to the flavor and bouquet of wine. Some of the polyphenols are apparently able to reduce blood-cholesterol levels.

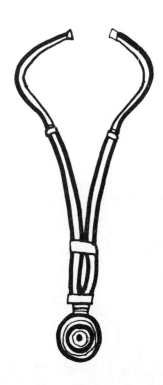

Other Uses of Wine in The Diet

We can rightfully judge wine to be not only the oldest dietary alcoholic beverage but the most important medicinal agent in continuous use throughout the history of man.

Wine is especially valuable when a tranquilizer has to be used over a long period of time, because its modest content of alcohol is not enough to create an unhealthy concentration of toxic materials in the body. We must also remember that many therapeutic agents are relatively insoluble in water, and that the minor amount of alcohol in wine renders it not only a safe solvent but a universal one.

In the diabetic diet, dry wines can serve not only as sources of energy but can enhance the flavor of a diet which is exceedingly bland and monotonous.

In diseases of the heart and circulatory system, wine is useful not only as a tranquilizer, but whenever a need exists to dilate the smaller blood vessels. It can enhance the dull diets of those suffering from heart disease or it can provide mild preventive measures against attacks of angina pectoris, which are due to the spasms of blood vessels within the heart. Recent studies suggest that wine in the daily diet may act as a protective factor against coronary disease.

In the care of the convalescent and especially of the aged, wine can help restore nutritional balance, relieve tensions, and serve not only as a gentle sedative but as an important euphoric agent.

When wine is used as a food with other foods at mealtime, it can help in developing cultural and sociological patterns aimed at the eradication of alcoholism.

Wine can be used advantageously during the early recovery period following an operation or a heart attack, and after natural childbirth—instances when the patient often is unable to accept solid food without experiencing nausea, or when his feeding must be restricted.

Never Forget Pleasure

The great 12th-century Jewish physician, Maimonides, said about wine, "It contains much good and light nourishment. It is rapidly digested and helps to digest other foods." He spoke the truth about wine as a utilitarian part of nutrition, but neglected a magical quality it possesses—the ability to give pleasure.

S. P. Lucia, M.D.

Food Calorie Chart

--A--

Almonds, shelled, whole, ¼ c 213
Anchovy
    Canned, 1 fillet.. 7
    Paste, 1 tsp. 14
Apple
    Baked (2 T. sugar), 1 med. 188
    Fresh, 1 med. 75
    Juice, bottled or canned, ½ c.................................. 60
Apple Betty, ½ c. 175
Apple butter, 1 T. 35
Applesauce, canned
    Sweetened, ½ c..115
    Unsweetened, ½ c. 50
Apricots
    Canned, calorie-reduced, ½ c. (av.) 46
    Canned, syrup-pack, ½ c..110
    Dried, cooked, unsweetened, ½ c. with juice 120
    Fresh (12 per lb.), 3 55
    Nectar, canned, ½ c. 70
Artichoke
    Canned, 1 heart (av.)... 7
    Fresh, Whole, 2 per lb., untrimmed, 1 50
    Frozen, hearts, 9-oz. pkg. 66
Asparagus, cooked or canned, 6 med. spears 25
Avocado, 10-oz. fruit, ½...185

--B--

Bacon, cooked crisp, 2 slices..................................... 92
    Canadian, cooked, 1 oz.. 79
Bagel, 3" diam., 1...165
Banana, 1 med. 100

Beans
    Baked, canned (pork & tomato sauce) 1 c...310
    Green, cooked, ½ c..15
    Kidney, canned or cooked, 1 c...230
    Lima, cooked, ½ c...95
Bean sprouts
    Cooked, ½ c..18
    Raw, ½ c..15
Beef, cooked
    Chipped or dried, 1 oz. 58
    Corned, canned, 3 oz. 185
    Corned beef hash, canned, 3 oz..155
    Flank steak, 3 oz. (av.) 183
    Ground, 3 oz. (av.)..216
    Rib Roast, 3 oz. (av.)..290
    Round or rump, 3 oz. (av.)..210
    Sirloin, 3 oz. (av.)..265
Beets, cooked, diced or sliced, ½ c...28
Beverages, alcoholic
    Beer, 12 fl. oz...150
    Gin, rum, vodka, whiskey
      80-proof, 1½ fl. oz. jigger 100
      86-proof, 1½ fl. oz. jigger 105
      90-proof, 1½ fl. oz. jigger 110
      94-proof, 1½ fl. oz. jigger 115
      100-proof, 1½ fl. oz. jigger 125
    Wines
      See Wine Calorie Chart, Page 109
Beverages, carbonated, sweetened, non-alcoholic
    Club soda, 12 fl. oz..0
    Cola type, 12 fl. oz..145
    Fruit-flavored sodas & Tom Collins mixes, 12 fl. oz............................170
    Ginger ale, 12 fl. oz..115
    Quinine or tonic water, 12 fl. oz...132
    Root beer, 12 fl. oz...150
Biscuits, baking powder, 2½" diam., 1...140
Blackberries, fresh, ½ c...40
Blueberries, fresh or unsweetened frozen, ½ c.......................................40
Bologna, sliced, 3" diam., ⅛" thick, 2 slices..80
Bouillon (beef broth) canned, condensed, 1 c..60
Bouillon cube (beef, chicken, vegetable), 1 cube 7
Bread, commercial (cracked wheat, French, raisin, rye, white, whole wheat),
    1 slice, (av.) 65
Broccoli, cooked, 2 small spears or ½ c. chopped 25
Brownies, with nuts, 2" sq., 1 90
Brussels sprouts, cooked, ½ c. 28
Butter, 1 T...100

--C--

Cabbage
  Shredded, cooked, ½ c. 15
  Shredded, raw, ½ c. 10
Cake
  Angel, 1/12 of 8″ cake 108
  Chocolate layer, chocolate frosting, 1/16 of 9″ cake 235
  Cupcake, 2½″, no icing... 90
  Fruit cake, 1/30 of 8″ loaf... 55
  Pound cake, 1 slice, ½″ thick 140
  Sponge cake, 1/12 of 10″ cake..195
  White layer, butter frosting, 1/16 of 9″ cake................................250
Candy
  Caramel, plain or chocolate, 1 oz...115
  Chocolate, milk, plain, 1 oz. 145
  Chocolate-coated peanuts, 1 oz..160
  Fudge, plain, 1 oz. 115
  Gumdrops, 1 oz..100
  Hard, 1 oz...110
  Peanut brittle, 1 oz...119
Cantaloupe, sm. to med., ½ ....50 to 60
Carrots
  Cooked, diced, ½ c. 25
  Raw, grated, ½ c... 22
Cashew nuts, roasted, ¼ c. 190
Catsup, 1 T. 18
Cauliflower
  Cooked flowerbuds, ½ c. 14
  Raw flowerbuds, ½ c. 11
Celery
  Cooked, diced, ½ c.. 11
  Raw, diced, ½ c. 10
  Raw, 1 lge. stalk 5
Cereal, cooked
  Cornmeal, yellow or white, 1 c. 120
  Farina, 1 c. 105
  Hominy grits, 1 c. 120
  Oatmeal, 1 c..130
Cereal, ready-to-eat
  Corn, rice, wheat flakes, 1 c. 100
  Puffed rice, wheat, 1 c. 55
  Shredded wheat, 1 lge. biscuit 90
Chard, cooked, ½ c... 17

Cheese
- American or Cheddar, natural, 1 oz......................115
- American or Cheddar, process, 1 oz.....................105
- Bleu or Roquefort, 1 oz...............................105
- Camembert, 1 oz.. 85
- Cottage, low-fat, 1 c.................................200
- Cream, 1 oz...105
- Edam, 1 oz..105
- Monterey Jack, 1 oz...................................103
- Mozzarella, 1 oz....................................... 84
- Neufchatel, 1 oz....................................... 73
- Parmesan, grated, 1 T.................................. 25
- Roquefort or Bleu, 1 oz...............................105
- Swiss, domestic, natural, 1 oz........................105
- Swiss, process, 1 oz..................................101

Cherries
- Canned, calorie-reduced, ½ c. (av.)................... 60
- Canned, syrup-pack, ½ c............................... 96
- Fresh, sweet or unsweetened frozen, ½ c............... 40

Chicken
- Breast, appr. 10 oz. raw weight, cooked, ½ 195
- Canned, boneless, ½ c................................200
- Cooked (simmered), diced, ½ c........................139
- Fryer, appr. 2¾ lbs. raw weight, cooked, ¼ 337

Chicken broth, canned, condensed, 1 c.................... 82
Chicken stock base, 1 tsp............................... 11

Chili con carne
- Canned, with beans, 1 c..............................332
- Canned, without beans, 1 c..........................510

Chili sauce, 1 T.. 16

Chocolate
- Bitter or baking, 1 oz...............................145
- Semi-sweet, 1 oz.....................................145
- Sweet, 1 oz..145
- Syrup, thin type, 1 oz............................... 70

Clams
- Canned, drained solids, 4 oz.........................111
- Canned, solids & liq., 4 oz.......................... 59
- Juice, bottled, 1 c.................................. 45

Cocoa
- Beverage, made with milk, 1 c........................245
- Powder, unsweetened, 1 T............................. 20

Coconut
- Dried, shredded, sweetened, ½ c......................252
- Fresh, grated or shredded, ½ c.......................225

Coffee, clear, 1 c...................................... 0
Consommé, canned, condensed, 1 c........................ 60

Cookies (packaged, commercial)
    Chocolate chip, 1 cookie 50
    Fig bar, 1 50
    Gingersnap, sm., 1 cookie 15
    Macaroon, 1 85
    Sandwich, chocolate or vanilla, 1 50
    Vanilla wafer, 1 15
Corn
    Canned, whole kernel, ½ c. 85
    Fresh, 1 ear, 5" x 1¾" 70
Corn chips, 1 oz. 164
Cornflake crumbs (packaged), 1 T 20
Cornstarch, 1 T 30
Crabmeat, canned, 3 oz. meat 85
Crackers
    Graham, 2½" sq., 2 crackers 55
    Oyster, ½ c. 60
    Round, "butter" type, 1 cracker 18
    Rye wafer, 1⅞" x 3½", 2 pieces 45
    Saltine, 4 crackers 50
    Soda, 2½" sq., 2 crackers 50
Cranberry juice cocktail, ½ c 83
Cranberry sauce, 1 T 25
Cream
    Half and half, 1 T. 20
    Heavy whipping, 1 T. 55
    Light, 1 T. 30
    Sour, commercial, 1 T. 25
Croutons, packaged, herb-seasoned, ½ c. 50
Cucumber, 6 slices, ⅛" thick 5
Custard, baked (reg. recipe), ½ c. 150

--D--

Danish pastry, no fruit or nuts, 4¼" diam. x 1" 275
Dates, pitted, cut, ¼ c. 125
Deviled ham, canned, 1 T. 45
Doughnut, cake type, 1 125

--E--

Egg, 1 lge. 80
    White only 15
    Yolk only 60
Eggplant, cooked, diced, ½ c. 19
Endive, curly, shredded, 1 c. 14
Escarole, shredded, 1 c. 14

--F--

--G--

--H--

--I--

--J--

Jam, 1 T. 55
Jelly, 1 T. 50

--K--

Kale, boiled, ½ c. 15
Kohlrabi, boiled, ½ c. 20

--L--

Lamb
   Chop (loin), appr. 5 oz. raw weight, cooked, lean only 122
   Leg, cooked, 3 oz. (av.) 204
Lard, 1 T. 115
Lemon, 1 med. 20
Lemon juice, 1 T. 4
Lemonade, frozen concentrate, diluted as directed, 1 c. 110
Lettuce
   Butter, ½ of a 7.8 oz. head 15
   Iceberg, ¼ of a 1-lb. head.. 15
   Iceberg, chopped, 1 c. 8
Liver
   Beef, fried, 3 oz. 195
   Calf, fried, 3 oz. 222
   Chicken, simmered, 3 oz. 141
Liver pâté, canned, 1 oz. 78
Liverwurst, 1 oz. 87
Lobster, meat only, cooked or canned, 4 oz...........................108

--M--

Macaroni, cooked, ½ c. 95
Macaroni and cheese
   Baked, 1 c. 430
   Canned, 1 c. 230
Maple syrup, 1 T. 50
Margarine
   Diet, 1 T. 51
   Regular, 1 T...100
Marmalade, 1 T. 55
Marshmallow, 1 oz. 90

Orange
  Fresh, sections, ½ c. 62
  Fresh, whole, 1 med. 60
  Juice, fresh, frozen, unsweetened canned, ½ c. 55
Oysters
  Canned, solids & liq., 4 oz. 86
  Raw, meat only, ½ c. 80

--P--

Pancakes, 1 (4″ av.) 60
Papaya, sm. to med., ½ ....50 to 60
Parsley, chopped, 1 T. 1
Parsnips, cooked, ½ c. 50
Peach
  Canned, calorie-reduced, ½ c. (av.) 36
  Canned, syrup-pack, ½ c. 100
  Fresh, sliced, 1 c. 65
  Fresh, whole, 1 med. to lge. ....50 to 60
  Frozen, sweetened, ½ c. 100
Peanut butter, 1 T. 95
Peanuts, roasted, salted halves, ¼ c. 210
Pear
  Canned, calorie-reduced, ½ c. (av.) 39
  Canned, syrup-pack, ½ c. 87
  Fresh, whole, 1 med. to lge. ....100 to 120
Peas, green
  Canned, drained, ½ c. 76
  Cooked, fresh / frozen, ½ c. (av.) 64
Pecans, halves, ¼ c. 185
Pepper
  Chili, canned, solids & liq., 4 oz. 28
  Green, raw, 1 med. 15
Persimmon, Japanese, 1 med. 77
Pickle relish, sweet, 1 T. 25
Pickles
  Dill, 1 med. (3¾″) 10
  Sweet, 1 sm. (2½″) 20
Pie, 4″ wedge, 1/7 of 9″ diam. pie
  Apple (2-crust)..350
  Butterscotch (1-crust) 350
  Cherry (2-crust)...350
  Custard (1-crust)..285
  Lemon meringue (1-crust) 305
  Mince (2-crust) 365
  Pecan (1-crust)...490
  Pumpkin (1-crust)...275

Pimiento, canned, 1 med. 10
Pineapple
    Canned, juice-pack, ½ c. chunks or 2 slices with 2 T. juice 64
    Canned, syrup-pack, ½ c. chunks or slices with 2 T. syrup 84
    Fresh, diced, ½ c. 40
    Juice, canned, unsweetened, ½ c. 70
Pizza, cheese, ⅛ of 14″ diam. pie 185
Plums
    Canned, calorie-reduced, ½ c. (av.) 58
    Canned, syrup-pack, ½ c. 100
    Fresh, 2″ diam., 1 25
Pomegranate, pulp & seeds, 1 med. 63
Popcorn, popped, with oil & salt, 1 c. 64
Popover, 1 av. 112
Pork, cooked
    Chop, 3 oz. without bone, lean only 230
    Loin, roasted, lean only, 3 oz. 219
Potato chips, 2″ diam., 10 chips 115
Potatoes
    Baked, 3 raw per lb., peeled after baking, 1 potato 92
    Boiled, 3 raw per lb., peeled after boiling, 1 potato 103
    French-fried, frozen, heated, 10 pieces 125
    Hash browned, ½ c. 230
    Mashed, with milk, ½ c. 63
    Sweet (yams)
        Baked or boiled, 1 med. (5″ x 2″) 160
        Candied, 3½″ x 2¼″, 1 295
        Canned, ½ c. 118
Pretzels
    Dutch, twisted, 1 pretzel 60
    Thin, twisted, 1 pretzel 25
Prune juice, canned or bottled, ½ c. 100
Prunes
    Cooked, unsweetened, ½ c. 148
    Dried, uncooked, 4 med. 70
Pumpkin, canned, 1 c. 80

--R--

Rabbit, cooked, meat only, 3 oz. 153
Radishes, sm., without tops, 4 5
Raisins, seedless, ½ c. 240
Raspberries, red, fresh, 1 c. 70
Rhubarb, cooked, sweetened, ½ c. 190
Rice
    Brown, cooked, ½ c. 100
    White, long-grain, cooked, ½ c. 91
Rock Cornish game hen, 1 lb. 6 oz. raw weight, roasted, ½ 312
Roll
    Hamburger or frankfurter 120
    Hard 160
Rusk, 1 piece 50
Rutabagas, cooked, diced, ½ c. 30

--S--

Salad dressing
    Bleu or Roquefort, 1 T. 75
    French, commercial, 1 T. 65
    Italian, 1 T. 85
    Mayonnaise, 1 T. 100
    Mayonnaise-type, 1 T. 65
    Thousand Island, 1 T. 80
Salad oil (see "Oil")
Salami, dry type, 1 oz. 130
Salmon
    Canned, pink, solids & liq., 4 oz. 160
    Canned, red, solids & liq., 4 oz. 194
    Fresh, baked or broiled, 4-oz. steak, (appr. 4" x 3" x ½") 206
Sardines, drained, 3 oz. 175
Sauerkraut, canned, ½ c. 20
Sausage, pork links, 16 per lb., cooked, 2 125
Scallops, cooked, 3 oz. 96
Sherbet, ½ c. 130
Shortening, vegetable, solid, 1 T. 110
Shrimp, canned, 3 oz. meat 100
Sole or flounder, cooked, 3 oz. 150
Soup, canned, condensed, diluted with water except where noted, 1 c.
    Asparagus, Cream of, with milk 144
    Asparagus, Cream of, with water 65
    Bean with Pork 170
    Beef Broth (Bouillon) or Consommé 30
    Beef Noddle 70
    Chicken, Cream of, with milk 180
    Chicken, Cream of, with water 95
    Chicken Noodle 65
    Chicken with Rice 50
    Clam Chowder (Manhattan) 80
    Celery, Cream of, with milk 166
    Celery, Cream of, with water 86
    Minestrone 105
    Mushroom, Cream of, with water 135
    Mushroom, Cream of, with milk 215
    Onion.. 65
    Pea, Green, with milk 208
    Pea, Green, with water 130
    Split Pea...145
    Tomato, Cream of, with milk 175
    Tomato, Cream of, with water 90
    Vegetable Beef 80

Soy Sauce, 1 T. 10
Spaghetti, cooked, ½ c. 108
Spinach
    Fresh, cooked, ½ c. 20
    Fresh, raw, cut for salad, 1 c. 14
    Frozen, chopped or leaf, 10-oz. pkg. 69
Squash, summer (zucchini, crookneck, pattypan),
    cooked, diced, ½ c. 15
Squash, winter, baked & mashed, ½ c. 65
Strawberries, capped, fresh or unsweetened frozen, 1 c. 53
Sugar
    Granulated or brown, 1 T. 50
    Powdered (confectioners'), 1 T. 30
Swordfish, cooked, 3 oz. 150
Syrup
    Corn, 1 T. 60
    Maple, 1 T. 50

--T--

Tangarine, med. (⅜" diam.), 1 40
Tea (no cream or sugar) 0
Tomato
    Canned, whole, solids & liq., ½ c. 25
    Fresh, med. (2" x 2½"), 1 tomato 33
    Juice, 1 c. 45
    Paste, 1 T. 12
    Sauce, 8-oz. can (av.) 75
    Stewed, 1-lb. can (av.) 129
Tortilla, corn
    5" diam., 1 tortilla 50
    6" diam., 1 tortilla 63
Tuna
    Packed in oil, drained solids, 6½-oz. can 294
    Packed in water or broth, drained solids, 6½-oz. can 225
Turkey, roasted, flesh & skin, 3 oz. 189
Turnips
    Cooked, diced, ½ c. 18
    Cooked, mashed, ½ c. 27

--V--

Veal, cooked, round or shoulder, 3 oz. (av.) 183
Vegetable juice cocktail, canned, 1 c. 45
Vienna sausage, 1 sausage 40
Vinegar, 1 T. 2

--W--

Waffle, 1 (7" diam.)..210
Walnuts, chopped, ¼ c. 200
Water chestnuts, 4 20
Watercress
    Sprigs, 10 2
    Trimmed, ½ c... 3
Watermelon
    Diced, 1 c.. 42
    Piece (4" x 8" with rind) 1..115
Worcestershire Sauce, 1 tsp.. 4

--Y--

Yams (see potatoes)
Yoghurt
    Fruit-flavored, 1 c. (av.)...250
    Plain, low-fat, 1 c. 120
    Plain, made from whole milk, 1 c................................150

--Z--

Zucchini, canned in tomato sauce, 1 c. 42
Zucchini, fresh (see Squash, summer)
Zwieback, 1 piece.. 30

Index to Diet, Wine, and Medical Terms

Index to Recipes

VEGETABLES